2PAC VS BIGGIE

AN ILLUSTRATED HISTORY OF RAP'S GREATEST BATTLE

D1614267

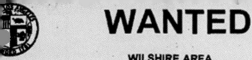

2PAC VS BIGGIE

AN ILLUSTRATED HISTORY OF RAP'S GREATEST BATTLE

JEFF WEISS AND EVAN MCGARVEY

First published in 2013 by Voyageur Press, an imprint of MBI Publishing Company, 400 First Avenue North, Suite 400, Minneapolis, MN 55401 USA

Voyageur Press titles are also available at discounts in bulk quantity for industrial or sales-promotional use. For details write to Special Sales Manager at MBI Publishing Company, 400 First Avenue North, Suite 400, Minneapolis, MN 55401 USA.

To find out more about our books, visit us online at www.voyageurpress.com.

ISBN-13: 978-0-7603-4367-8

Library of Congress Cataloging-in-Publication Data

McGarvey, Evan, 1984-
  2pac v. Biggie : an illustrated history of rap's greatest battle / Evan McGarvey and Jeff Weiss.
    p. cm.
  Includes bibliographical references.
  ISBN 978-0-7603-4367-8 (softcover)
  1. Shakur, Tupac, 1971-1996. 2. Notorious B.I.G., 1972-1997. 3. Rap musicians--United States--Biography. 4. Rap (Music)--History and criticism. I. Weiss, Jeff, 1981- II. Title. III. Title: Tupac v. Biggie. IV. Title: 2pac versus Biggie. V. Title: Tupac versus Biggie.
  ML420.S529M34 2013
  782.421649092'2--dc23
  [B]
                                    2012040556

Cover: (left) Scott Gries / Getty Images, (right) Ferdaus Shamim / WireImage / Getty Images Back flap: *Pac and Big*, by Reuben Cheatem. *Courtesy of the artist.* Frontis: *Tupac Shakur* (left) and *The Notorious B.I.G.* (right), by Jordan Zehner. Stencil on newspaper. *Courtesy of the artist;* Page 8: *Legends Together*, by Matt Burke. Oil painting, 2009. Features The Notorious B.I.G., 2Pac, Eminem, Dr. Dre, T.I., Lil Wayne, and Kanye West. *Courtesy of the artist*

Editor: Grace Labatt
Design Manager: James Kegley
Layout: Kim Winscher
Page designer: Sandra Salamony

Printed in China

10 9 8 7 6 5 4 3 2 1

To my parents—for everything, but especially
for never asking to hear what I was listening to.
— Jeff Weiss

For Allegra
"Things to make you smile; what numbers to dial
You gon' be here for a while?"
— Evan McGarvey

CONTENTS

PREFACE

Less than two decades after the deaths of Tupac Shakur and Christopher Wallace, it has become impossible to speak one name without hearing the other. 2Pac and Biggie. Biggie and 2Pac. You see a poster of one and think of an image of the other. You get to know a friend, a fellow rap fan, and you ask whom they prefer. It feels natural when a party's soundtrack moves from the fizzy, delirious "California Love" to the elemental bass of "Hypnotize." Biggie and 2Pac. 2Pac and Biggie.

They died six months apart. Tupac was murdered in September of 1996, Biggie in March of 1997. Since then, their complicated bond has ossified in our social memory. The ampersand, the ellipsis, the "vs."—whatever link now appears in our mind when we think about 2Pac and Biggie is due for complication. This book is an attempt to provide listeners, new and old, with fresh angles for appreciating The Notorious B.I.G. and 2Pac. (Throughout the book, "Tupac" will refer to the person, "2Pac"—his rap name—to the artist.)

They were dynamic men, driven self-inventors and iconoclasts. Born a chubby, doted-upon only child, Biggie became a dapper hip-hop don with a visceral, visual imagination and a voice like cavalry riding across marble. 2Pac was a reedy art-school student who transformed himself into the most famous poet-provocateur-outlaw this side of Rimbaud. Both served as the faces of industry-shaking record labels. Both ushered rap into the era of pyrotechnic music videos, pop dominance, and global audiences.

But why Biggie and 2Pac? While subversive, neither rapper made the most transgressive songs of the era. Each had massive commercial success, but neither cut a particularly pop-friendly figure. However, as different as they were in appearance, biography, and temperament, they shared one magnificent quality: the ability to synthesize an assortment of artistic virtues into a singular, irresistible presentation.

Where Biggie became a master of genre and perspective and detail, 2Pac created rhetoric that could champion sprawling spirituality and triumphant cooperation in one moment and fierce self-preservation and fatalism in the next. They did not merely emphasize their strengths as MCs and rappers and performers; they each created a verbal universe. For this kind of artistic fulfillment to happen once in a generation is an event. For it to happen to two artists, and for the artists not only to know one another but also to find their work in dialogue and their lives woven together with threads of camaraderie, betrayal, and death, is monumental.

The books about the two are many. In particular, the time from Tupac's criminal trial in 1994 until Biggie's murder in 1997 has been examined, researched, and argued endlessly. But this book aims to bring fresh perspective to the irreducible core of 2Pac and Biggie's shared legacy: the music. After all, music—seminal albums, unforgettable singles, and apocryphal early recordings—is what they have left behind. We examine Biggie and 2Pac individually, talk about each stage in their lives and how each rendered that chapter or theme into music. Their subjects were the timeless subjects of American pop music: childhood, adolescence, love, sex, getting rich, staying rich, family, friendship, hate, work, play, choice, fate. And the lyrical routes each took across this terrain reflect their identities as artists. The instances of consonance thrill: a creeping paranoia infuses both 2Pac's "All Eyez On Me" and Biggie's "My Downfall." The instances of separation instruct. Compare the two approaches to biography in 2Pac's sympathetic, humane "Dear Mama" and in Biggie's clinical, systematic "Sky's The Limit." Their lyrical approaches, song structures, storytelling habits, vocabularies, cadences, engagements with big human themes—these are what make Biggie and 2Pac so endlessly fascinating, so rewarding to hear individually and in contrast.

We are fascinated by Biggie and 2Pac because the cultural moment in which we live is part of their legacy. Hip-hop has become pop. The art of rap has influenced singers, songwriters, and producers in every genre of popular music. A hundred would-be rappers use manufactured "beef" to try to drum up record sales. The line between performer and performance was always permeable and useful, but Biggie and 2Pac made it threatening. Academia has taken up both men as subjects of study. 2Pac's face appears on murals in ghettos, favelas, and shantytowns around the world. Biggie's phrases nestle in sitcom scripts and news teleprompters. A decade after Biggie documented the bloodless exchange of human dreams for crude capital in his album *Life After Death*, we lived through a financial meltdown that felt very much like one of his unflinching narratives. A decade after we heard 2Pac rap, "We ain't ready to see a black president," we elected one.

We can't separate them. We shouldn't. They move like neighboring constellations across an American night sky. We may momentarily lose sight of one as we gaze at the other, but we cannot appreciate them alone. The poet and the orator. The line and the circle. The Atlantic and the Pacific. 2Pac and Biggie. Biggie and 2Pac.

Chapter 1

dytodie  notorio

PORTRAITS OF THE ARTISTS AS YOUNG MEN

2PAC

From the womb to the tomb, Tupac Amaru Shakur was both royalty and outlaw. His  first screams shattered no calm on June 16, 1971—one month after his Black Panther mother was acquitted of conspiring to murder New York City cops and dynamite five Midtown department stores, a police precinct, six railroad rights of way, and the New York Botanical Gardens. Even in utero, his soundtrack was the slamming of cell doors and the yells of the dispossessed. During his embryonic phase, his world was a desolate hollow of hunger pains and pounding gavels.

Black Panther convention at the Lincoln Memorial, 1970. *PHOTOGRAPH BY THOMAS J. O'HALLORAN AND WARREN K. LEFFLER. LIBRARY OF CONGRESS*

Afeni, arrested for a plot to bomb five Manhattan department stores.
ASSOCIATED PRESS

Shakur's birth certificate read Lesane Parish Crooks, but within thirty-six months he'd been renamed for the last Incan emperor, a rebel beheaded by the Spanish before thousands in Cuzco in modern-day Peru. The fact that they met similar ends was no accident of irony. From birth, Tupac was bred for resistance—though not necessarily for the thug life. In fact, his rap sheet didn't begin until long after he'd already been famous. Yet his embrace of the outlaw myth was practically chemical instinct. So it goes when your godfather is Geronimo Pratt and your godmother is Assata Shakur, both prominent activists and Black Panthers. Though less celebrated than many of her would-be revolutionary peers, Afeni had her high-profile supporters: her $100,000 bail was partially footed by Leonard Bernstein and Jane Fonda.

This was the uptown Manhattan of "radical chic." The utopian ideals of the 1960s had hardened into active resistance in the wake of the assassinations. With Richard Nixon in the White House, Afeni Shakur bounced from job to job and apartment to apartment, initially living off of speaking fees at universities (including one engagement at Harvard). Though she may have briefly burnished the pseudo-street cred of the uptown elite, as the 1970s progressed, Afeni fell prey to hard drugs and empty bank accounts. For all of his identification with the wide-open west, Tupac spent his formative years in the New York crucible, compressed between couches in roach-infested apartments and homeless shelters, alongside his mom and younger sister.

Like Biggie, Tupac was raised in the cradle of hip-hop during the genre's chief years of gestation. It was the sound of the New York City streets, and young Tupac was obviously immersed in the 4/4 rhythms and brittle electronic drum machines of the old school. However, it was Black Panther philosophy and *The Autobiography of Malcolm X* that really galvanized his consciousness. Later on, he claimed that growing up, "Black Power was a lullaby."

Listening to 2Pac's catalog is like staring at an X-ray—it reveals an astonishingly complex architecture but two-toned coloration. 2Pac leaves no room for equivocation. Holler if you hear him or he will fuck you up. He derives his power from being able to inspire passion in the normally stolid. He is a rap wedge issue, the archetypal sensitive thug, an intellectual who wanted peace and violence and always fell victim to blunted damned paranoia. He could be everything or nothing—whatever angle you wanted to approach from. So from Venice Beach to sub-Saharan Africa, his face is on T-shirts at every tacky souvenir shop, permanently stained in the pop culture firmament like Jim Morrison, Tony Montana, or Kurt Cobain. Live fast, die young, and leave a gangsta-looking corpse, bullet-riddled for the paparazzi age. He sublimated the struggle of his race but simplified his message to make it accessible to anyone alienated, isolated, or angry. No one has ever channeled fury quite like 2Pac. He exists not as the patron saint of one region, but as a populist revolutionary, martyred for muddled causes.

Before the self-destruction, there was the vulnerable child with a large smile and long eyelashes, one who loved poetry and theater and learned to cook and sew. His cousins chided him for his delicate features and lack of athletic ability. Tupac was raised in the hood, but he wasn't a street hood. He was the product of an impoverished and infamous elite: his stepfather Mutulu Shakur was an eccentric radical aligned with the Weathermen, who operated something called the Black Acupuncture Advisory Association of North America out of a brownstone deep uptown.

Eventually, allegedly, Mutulu graduated to robbing armored cars and banks under the auspices of a criminal organization known as The Family. After five years on the run as one of the FBI's Ten Most Wanted, Shakur was nabbed in 1986. Tupac was fifteen and had been frequently haunted over the last half decade by visits from federal agents attempting to know whether or not he'd seen his stepfather. His next father figure, Legs, was tied to the powerful gangs of Nicky Barnes, immortalized in the film *American Gangster*. The shy, quiet boy absorbed the loaded dice swagger of the uptown drug runner until Legs, too, was imprisoned, on charges of credit card fraud. Legs died a few years later in prison, an event that reportedly severely affected the mercurial Tupac, who claimed that the thug life side of his personality came from having refracted the diamond-studded cool of Legs.

The distrust and edge in 2Pac's music might have been amplified by his adult encounters with authority, but those qualities were instilled from day one. His early instability, radical surroundings, and constant transience lent him a tremendous sense of empathy. He understood how to act around intellectuals and high society, but endured a childhood of always being the new kid who was forced to impress. By nature, his relationships were ephemeral; he had to be ready to move at any time. And his musical style reflects that: it's restless, rambling, and filled with as many impassioned run-ons as a Kerouac novel. For 2Pac, the writing is in service to the idea.

A chief bright spot of his early years was his apprenticeship in the 127th Street Repertory Ensemble, where he played Travis in a production of *A Raisin in the Sun*. It laid the groundwork for his high school years as a drama major at the Baltimore School for the Arts. At heart, 2Pac was a chameleon, an actor able to assimilate any style or role. While in Baltimore, he rapped under

Young Tupac.
© PARAMOUNT PICTURES / COURTESY EVERETT COLLECTION

the name MC New York, boasting an image diametrically opposed to the thugged-out rider killed on a broiling night in Las Vegas. In the mid-1980s, he rocked a high-top fade haircut and boho-hippie garb. His best friends were Jada Pinkett and a rich white kid named John Cole. When he was ten years old, Tupac told a preacher that he wanted to be a revolutionary. By the time he was fifteen, his naturally theatrical instincts guided him to perform the plays of Shakespeare. He was essentially an art-school kid who might have found his way into a top-tier acting program had his mom not opted to leave the state upon receiving an eviction notice.

After Tupac's death, a collection of poems from his early years surfaced, most of which were composed in Baltimore. Despite their relative lack of literary merit, the poems are a revelatory document of biographical import. In "In the Depths of Solitude," he's "trying to find peace of mind and still preserve [his] soul," a "young heart with an old soul." Even as a teenager, Tupac was grappling with the ideas of art versus commerce and he importance of authenticity. They would be the same demons that he'd face after signing with Death Row—how to appease his inner revolutionary

"Now who's to say if I was right or wrong? / To live my life as an outlaw all along / Remain strong in this planet full of playa haters / They conversate, but Death Row full of demonstrators."

– "Until the End of Time"

while still living up to the thug life image that earned platinum plaques, the total respect of the streets, and enough scarred sensitivity to garner him a female fan base that even LL Cool J had to envy.

Later in the same poem, Tupac writes, "how can I be in the depths of solitude when there are two inside me / this duo within me causes / the perfect opportunity / to learn and live twice as fast / as those who accept simplicity."

By the time he was old enough to drive, Tupac had knowledge of self. His destiny was already scribbled into an old notebook preserved through countless moves and perennial tumult. There are no analogues for 2Pac in rap. He is the literary aspirant who gained gravity not by the words themselves, but through the weary baritone conviction shrouding their vocals. His closest musical antecedent is Jim Morrison, a mix of boorishness, brilliance, and unfiltered emotion.

If you don't believe 2Pac, you can't like 2Pac. If you buy the image, the attitude, and share an instinctual compulsion to smite your enemies in biblical fashion, 2Pac is likely to be your favorite rapper. Ask a group of 2Pac fans why he's the best and they will rarely give you a good answer. You can point to the complexity that has inspired college courses. You can point to the sprawling catalog that continues to trickle out music even a decade and a half after his death. But the truth is that there's no one tangible reason. Loving 2Pac is like believing in a religion—you have to take a massive leap of faith and just believe. His secret is that he hits people on a raw, primal level. His energy was enormous. When you listen to his songs, you know him; you feel his pain and understand the plot points of his story without having to have them spelled out.

Much of 2Pac's catalog is short on tracks specifically grounded in the details of his upbringing. He's less interested in telling his story than in articulating universal themes of being trapped, vulnerable, and vengeful. His history trickles out in asides and rarely through the involute narratives favored by Biggie. Yet many of 2Pac's most powerful songs are narratives, none more lionized than "Dear Mama," the Mother's Day rap anthem that was inducted into the Library of Congress National Recording Registry.

Not only did "Dear Mama" mint a veritable subgenre of rappers making songs about how much they love their mothers, it remains the gold standard by which all of them are judged. The song plays like a more linear version of his poetry set to music. The rhyme scheme is simple: AABB. The lyrics are direct and uncomplicated, and the story is little different than millions of

Tupac v. Warhol, by Leon Kaye. Spray paint and hand-cut stencils, 2009.

others. And admittedly, it can be saccharine in its straightforwardness, but it also derives an immense power from this same forthrightness.

In "Dear Mama," 2Pac is seventeen and fighting with his mom. She kicks him out. She provides for him in spite of her debilitating crack addiction. He recognizes his debt can never be repaid. But it's the way in which he almost sings each bar, hanging on the last syllables like he's tattooing his mom's name on his abdomen—it's a silly but sweet gesture that may seem overwrought, but unlike humor and irony, sincerity and straightforwardness can easily transcend generational ticks and trends.

There are some things you can't fake. Even at the height of their beef, The Notorious B.I.G. declared 2Pac "the realest rapper out." Eliding his revolutionary bloodline, it was 2Pac's sense of conviction that caused him his messianic appeal. Listening to "Dear Mama" triggers long-buried sepia home movies of you and your mother, the ones that were never filmed. Suddenly, your own shortcomings are bathed in an unflattering light— you remember a phone call never made, an opportunity only given because of what your mother sacrificed for you. 2Pac will keep you honest.

1992.
TIME LIFE PICTURES / GETTY IMAGES

Pac and Big, by Reuben Cheatem. Acrylic on canvas, 2011. "This painting was intentionally designed to perpetuate the debate of which rapper should be considered the sole holder of the title, the indisputable greatest legend in the hip hop genre.... The painting has no clear distinction of whose face is in the foreground and whose lies behind the other. It also uses equal balance and weight with the color and sizing of each artist's face, so no 'winner' is represented. Moreover, it is a subtle statement against the conflict that led to the untimely deaths of both men. The color palette and close proximity of their faces denote a level of peace that was never achieved between them in their lifetime." —Cheatem
COURTESY OF THE ARTIST

BIGGIE

EVAN MCGARVEY

First the Indians. Then the Dutch. Then the English. Then the world. That, in brief, rough order, is the list of New York City's owners. And since the seventeenth century, when Peg Leg Pete Stuyvesant built the wall on Wall Street (originally for defense, quickly employed by local merchants as a trading post), each immigrant wave has brought its own heady mix of narratives and languages, of foods and clothes and, well, stuff, to the islands, inlets, and parks of the five boroughs. Clichés? Yes. Canards? Hardly. In the twentieth century, the tidal forces of immigration intensified. There were decades when half the NYPD was Irish. When the WASP law firms thought "hostile takeovers" were uncouth for men of Exeter and Harvard, the Jewish firms, built by the children of Poland and Russia and Germany, filled that white-collar vacuum. The Great Migration brought a new network of churches, social organizations, and black-owned businesses to Harlem. The first generation arrives, labors, and dies. It is the children—the children of Irish patrolmen, of Chinese restaurant owners on Ludlow, of Ghanaian shopkeepers south of Prospect Park, of salon owners on 125th Street—who rechristen the machinery of the concrete jungle each and every New York morning. The children get to live the dream of the city.

Voletta Wallace was born in Jamaica. In 1968, not yet twenty, she immigrated to New York. The country she left behind resembled so many other New York immigrants' homelands—newly independent from its colonial overlord, suffering from the throws of rapid class separation, violent crime, and clamped-down social mobility. Yet the New York she found was undergoing changes of its own. MLK, Malcolm X, and the Kennedy brothers: all dead. The Tet Offensive: ongoing. Hispanic and Afro-Caribbean immigrants who had arrived in New York since the dawn of the twentieth century had reshaped both the Bronx—where Voletta first arrived—and Brooklyn, where she later settled. The surge of heavy industrial jobs, like those in the Brooklyn Navy Yard, which had employed so many of those men, waned. In Brooklyn, Edith Wharton–era mansions stood around the corner from row homes and tenements. A better life was there but hardly guaranteed.

Christopher Wallace, son of Voletta and George Latore (also Jamaican-born, decades older than Voletta, harboring a second family in London), was born May 21, 1972. On the opening track ("Intro") of his debut, 1994's *Ready To Die*, The Notorious B.I.G. renders his own birth as not just the literal labor pains of his mother (with Sean Combs providing the voice of

the cheerleading father), but through a sort of "dawn of man" soundtrack. The iconic bass ripples of Curtis Mayfield's "Superfly" give way to "Rapper's Delight," the latter providing the background for his "parents'" argument about young Biggie's shoplifting. Here he charts his artistic birth as borne from life experience and crime.

Ready To Die's lead single, "Juicy," provides the foundation for Biggie's self-mythologizing. Worthy of all its plaudits as one of the 1990s' definitive, seminal, and simply best songs, "Juicy" compels because of how different the childhood Biggie describes in the song is from Christopher Wallace's. As Voletta Wallace detailed in her extensive interview with Cheo Hodari Coker for *Unbelievable: The Life, Death and Afterlife of The Notorious B.I.G.* (2003, Three Rivers Press), young Christopher's life was far from "sardines for dinner." The doted-upon only child raised on the solidly working-class street of St. James Place in Clinton Hill had, according to Voletta, stereos, a color television, and all three video game systems: Atari, Intellivision, and ColecoVision. Though far from cushy, his life resembled that of many other only children of New York immigrants: protected, perpetually monitored, and aware of each material improvement in the family's status. He had candy. His mother let him stay inside and watch television all day. As Voletta has testified, she took Christopher back to Jamaica each summer, providing him with something that many of his second-generation immigrant peers lacked: a vivid connection to his ancestral land. He absorbed Jamaica's sights, stories, and linguistic rhythms. And back home in Brooklyn, he was a 1980s baby; he did not have to work in a factory or in a mine—which makes the spiritual truths and material fictions of "Juicy" all the more resonant.

The song's first verse gives us a picture of Biggie as fan, as listener: "I used to read up *Word Up Magazine:* / Salt-n-Pepa; Heavy D up in the limousine. / Hanging pictures on my wall, / every Saturday: Rap attack Mr. Magic, Marley Marl. / I let my tape rock till my tape popped." While the bulk of the song covers Biggie's young adulthood, the time when he was indeed a broke young drug dealer, these opening lines, some of the most evocative childhood lyrics in hip-hop, capture not the birth of the young artist, but the adoration of the might-be artist gazing at his idols. It's the debut of the listener, not of the rapper. He's quite literally just like us. Again separating himself from 2Pac, he sees himself as a boy developing into fan into hustler into man, not as a prophet to be received by the world.

Also unlike 2Pac, who rarely mentioned the names of rappers before him, the first verse explicitly names influences. Like a poet, he evokes not just the muse, but also the names of the old masters who inspired his pursuit of craft. Read those lyrics again. Biggie constructs the routine of the disciple: layering up posters, naming the idols, popping his tapes like a Catholic thumbs a rosary or a Muslim kneels on a kilim. That sense of apprenticeship flashes in other Biggie songs. But they are just flashes.

As a lyricist, Biggie often compressed entire stretches of time into a deft turn of phrase while expanding a single moment into an entire verse—all in the same song. Biggie renders childhood itself—a generalized set of imagined experiences—rather than the actual circumstances of Christopher Wallace. The actual young man becomes Biggie the stick-up wizard, Biggie the hustler, Biggie the lyrical artisan.

His early life was determined by a shift from the academy to the streets. Like Tupac, Wallace came from a family that deeply valued education. Voletta had a master's degree from Brooklyn College and worked in early childhood education in New York. Her supremely diligent parenting and the strong parochial options in Brooklyn offered Christopher Wallace his first game to master: school. The oral histories in Coker's *Unbelievable* tell the story of a young prodigy: a sweet, spoiled young boy who could talk a classmate out of his lunch at Quincy-Lexington Open Door Day Care, race through the alphabet and dash off basic arithmetic at the Catholic St. Peter Claver Elementary, and charge his friends a quarter each to use the video games at his house.

Voletta shielded her son against the specter of dangerous neighborhood influences. Like the speaker in "Juicy" watching his rap heroes live a life he could only imagine, Wallace spent his childhood watching the young bucks only a few years older than him dipping into the dark side of adolescence in do-or-die Bed-Stuy. For a rapper who wielded an eye that peerlessly balanced minute detail and cinematic scope, Brooklyn afternoons, when the fading light glinted off cars, sneakers, windows, puddles, and faces, supplied a trove of images for the ambitious young man trapped watching it all from his mother's stoop. Observant children become artists. They learn from youth that details compose the world. The lonely, insular life of the only child creates craving for the image and the system. Soon enough the system of childhood, the school, would give way to the system of adolescence—the street.

The soft yellows and stately blues of his parochial school uniforms would soon became old relics. Biggie had attended the private middle

Juicy Coogi, by Tony Duman. Acrylic spray paint and paint markers on canvas, 2012.
COURTESY OF THE ARTIST

school Queen of All Saints and the famed Bishop Loughlin Memorial High School (Rudy Giuliani's alma mater). For Voletta, who worked two jobs to keep them in the comfortable spot on St. James and keep Christopher in private school, this was the track of education, achievement, and success for which so many New York immigrants worked. Her son saw things differently. The street life of Brooklyn and its hypnotic material features—fresh clothes, street hustles, hints of fast, unlimited wealth—spoke to her son like a new language. And he could not study that language in the docile, lawyer/teacher/CPA factory of Brooklyn's private schools. Biggie requested a transfer to Westinghouse High School (now the George Westinghouse Career and Technical Education High School), a nearby P.S. outpost. The little prince of St. James Place would get his wish to mix with the rabble of his generation and live that much closer to street level.

The school became a catalyst for long-simmering trends. His attitude shifted from fresh to defiant. He challenged teachers and coasted on his natural gifts for rhetoric, rhyme, and mathematics. His burning desire for stuff—money, clothes, and general material ease—supplanted his scholarly gifts. Voletta hoped he might become an artist one day; as a boy, Christopher would replicate pictures he saw with a nearly perfect freehand

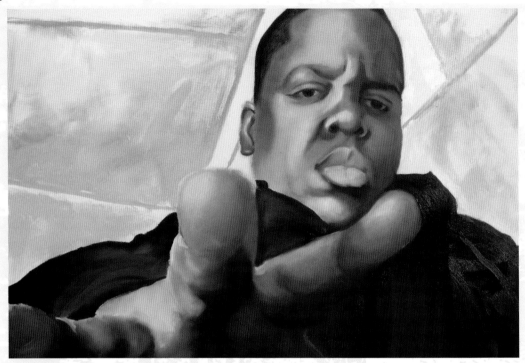

***Hypnotize*, by Matt Burke.** *COURTESY OF THE ARTIST*

sketch. The prestigious Pratt Institute was blocks away from the family home. But Biggie picked up his true calling through the osmosis of the streets. Now a young adolescent coming of age in the throes of the Reagan era, Biggie saw that there was one way, and one way only, that the young men around him were getting the Polo, Adidas, Lacoste, and gold fronts. New York, like L.A., Chicago, Miami, and D.C., belonged to crack cocaine.

The gates of childhood swung shut behind Biggie. The crack game would bring Christopher Wallace the stripes of adulthood and authenticity he so craved. His mother's immigrant wishes for the success of her child were to be subverted. The canvas on which Biggie would first work would be the street, and the tight Brooklyn childhood that his mother worked so hard to give him would rupture into the world at large.

Perhaps the fullest record of this moment occurs during "Sky's The Limit," from his tragically posthumous magisterial *Life After Death* double album. Here, unlike on "Juicy," Biggie supplies images of a childhood that more accurately matches his own experience. He portrays himself as a young man fueled by material desire, going so far as to forge his own faux luxury-brand polo shirts, "sewing tigers on my shirt, and alligators. / You wanna see the inside? I see ya later." The song opens with an imagined convocation from his "mother" before the mother's prologue turns into the voice of the artist as a master of ceremonies introducing himself. The psychological imagery is rich. As Biggie closes the first verse, itself an elegy for young adolescent idealism and pratfalls (people do, in fact, realize that the speaker's shirts are fakes), he turns from the simple, stable childhood pleasure of friends sharing snacks to the tenuous relationships that exist around a young drug dealer: "I mean loyalty: niggas bought me milks at lunch. / Them milks was chocolate; the cookies, butter crunch… / In here, eyes crossed from blue and white dust / Pass the blunt."

Childhood was over. All was but prologue.

"Dead leaders for a dead system"

Chapter 2

WHERE THEY CAME FROM WHERE THEY WENT

2PAC

Picture Pac rolling. The jangled clatter of public transit substituted by the sumptuous glide of 500 Benzes. Midnight Greyhound shambles replaced with first-class flights and bittersweet Cristal. There were eighteen changes of residence during Tupac's first decade, as he rotated among Manhattan and the outer boroughs. His formative memories were molded by a dirty blur of claustrophobic tenements and empty refrigerators.

There were subsequent relocations and reimaginations in Baltimore, the Bay Area, and Los Angeles. He even kept a home in Atlanta, long before it became a third capital of the hip-hop industry. With the exception of his exile at the Clinton Correctional Facility, the only constant was constant motion.

The American imagination is prone to myth and tall tale: Paul Bunyan and Pecos Bill; Casey Jones and John Henry. 2Pac was closest to the latter: proudly black, indefatigable, and with a penchant for unfortunate overall choices. Both were only stopped by steel. Each was the modern manifestation of the African-American diaspora—forever in flux and at the mercy of any glint of economic opportunity. While Biggie had to shift weight in the Carolinas to understand the moonshine-medicated imbalances of the South, Tupac's ancestors hailed from the country of tobacco fields and Jesse Helms. As Tayannah Lee McQuillar notes in *Tupac Shakur: The Life and Times of An American Icon*, the rapper was raised on stories about the rebellion of the Lumbee Indians of Lumberton, North Carolina, a tribe that recruited recently freed slaves from the countryside to aid them in their seven-year guerilla war against the white planter aristocracy.

A survey that aired on PBS's *African-American Lives* estimated that 58 percent of African Americans have the racial equivalent of at least one white great-grandparent. In line with the majority, Tupac's great-great grandfather was an indigent white man from Lumberton named Powell. When he married a devout black woman named Millie Ann in 1892, his punishment

Tupac N America, by Walter O. Neal.
Digital art print, 2010. *COURTESY OF THE ARTIST*

was familial excommunication and the indignity of being bound to a covered wagon and forcibly dragged through town. Descended from Afro-Jamaican stock, Biggie was rooted to the Big Apple, a classical avatar of the American immigrant experience—pure Horatio Alger. But Tupac was a product of the struggle, a transatlantic trail of tears sublimated into every stanza.

Listen to Afeni Shakur bear witness to the blunt impact of a 1958 uprising during which the Lumbee drove the Klan out of Lumberton (from *Afeni Shakur: Evolution of a Revolutionary*): "Klan came in and tried to impose a ten o' clock curfew on the Indian and Black Community . . . posted notices up about race mixing. . . . So the Klan had a rally posted . . . the Lumbees got guns and rifles and ambushed the Klan at their own rally. . . . Those white-hooded crackers ran into the woods like the little wing wangs they were. . . . That was my first taste of resistance."

The land that Tupac stalked was this cartography of resistance.

A Blues for Tupac, by Harold Smith. Mixed media on fiber board (oil and printed media), 2010. Collection of **Mr. Robert Brown.** *COURTESY OF THE ARTIST*

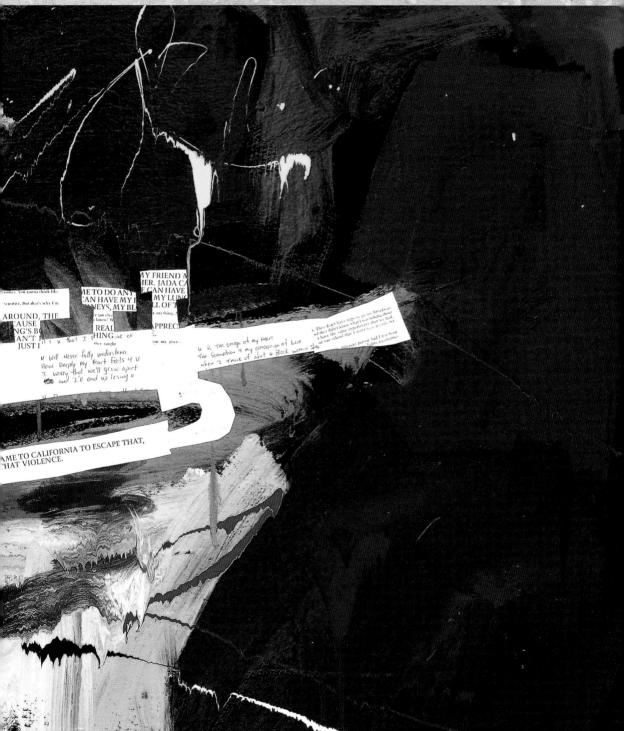

Like many African Americans whose families experienced the racial cruelty of the South, Tupac grew up hearing sagas of bigotry and rebellion. He was not tied to one place, but was wedded to his people, haunted by the systematic burden of hundreds of years of forced transit and broken bonds. For him, metropolitan detail was incidental. His chief concern was the infected marrow of city and state. Few of his early songs are more specific than "Trapped," in which he diagrams the contrast between institutional oppression and the imperative of freedom:

> They got me trapped.
> Can barely walk the city streets
> Without a cop harassing me, searching me
> Then asking my identity
> Hands up, throw me up against the wall
> Didn't do a thing at all
> I'm telling you one day these suckers gotta fall.

2Pac's first studio album, 1991.

The hook roars in repetition: "They got us trapped, nah, can't keep the black man down." The brilliance of 2Pac lies in his ability to capture the universality of the American black experience. Sometimes there are fancy ways to illustrate a point, and other times, it's far more effective just to say: "I Don't Give a Fuck." That was the name of another of the most searing songs from *2Pacalypse Now*, in which 2Pac's outro offers "fuck offs" to all his enemies at that moment: the San Francisco Police Department, the Marin County Sheriff's Department, the FBI, the CIA, the "B-U-S-H," "the AmeriKKKa," and "all redneck prejudiced motherfuckers." You didn't have to be from the Bay to empathize. These were late-twentieth-century parables of rebellion, the counterpart to oral histories of antebellum ambushes.

But the legend started to metastasize in Northern California. Tupac's stable respite at the Baltimore School for the Arts was shattered when his mother was evicted, forcing Shakur and his younger sister, Sekyiwa, to leave Maryland for Marin City, just north of San Francisco. According to lore, a seventeen-year-old Tupac boarded the cross-country bus with just five dollars in his pocket and four chicken wings. In "the jungle," he fell into the street life, soaking up game from pushers and pimps and criminals. Crack, coke, and weed were everywhere. Afeni was hooked. Trapped between polarities, Tupac was dead broke, hustling, and trying to forge a rap career, while simultaneously describing himself as the target for street gangs. He thought he was "weird for writing poetry. . . . I hated myself. I was really a nerd."

The reinvention began with Digital Underground. Through an introduction procured by his first manager and mentor, Leila Steinberg, 2Pac wound up in the studio during the mixing of the group's platinum debut, *Sex Packets*. Impressed with his raw talent and intensity, D.U. leader Gregory "Shock G" Jacobs inducted the teenager into the funkadelic circus.

Initially a backup dancer, Shakur's ability and persistence won him a place on "Same Song," a single from Digital Underground's *This is an EP Release* (1991). Much like Biggie's introduction, "Party and Bullshit," it was a straightforward party-starter. But in only sixteen bars ostensibly dedicated to groupies, 2Pac reveals his personal paradoxes: the struggle between staying true or giving in to the indulgences of fame, his attraction to and repulsion from the fickle women who paid him no mind before he joined the biggest Bay Area rap group of the early 1990s. The nice guy and the nerd were already starting to dissolve into the acidity of the outlaw immortal.

2Pacalypse Now rifles between traditional East Coast boom-bap and the Bay Bridge funk of Digital Underground. It operates as a nexus between the Afrocentric militancy of Public Enemy, Paris, and X-Clan and the nihilistic pre-riot rage of N.W.A. 2Pac's geographic sensibilities existed in his mind. He couldn't claim to be Straight Outta Compton, but he understood that by articulating the mentality of ghetto life, he could touch anyone in duress. It was the inverse of Tolstoy: everyone in his unhappy clan resembled each other.

Nothing better illustrated this idea than the decision to make "Brenda's Got a Baby" his first official single. Inspired by a story he saw in the newspaper, 2Pac wrote a harrowing requiem for a twelve-year-old girl knocked up by her older molester cousin. After briefly abandoning the baby in a trash bin, she reconsiders and opts to raise the child by any means necessary. Since she can "barely spell her name," she attempts to sell crack, but gets robbed. Finally forced to sell sex, she winds up a lurid headline: "Prostitute found slain and Brenda's her name."

It could have happened in any hood, but the bedrock was the Bay, still aflame from the ravages of Reaganomics and the crack trade. Cokeland was its unofficial alias at the time. And 2Pac was careful to acknowledge his adopted hometown on "Rebel from the Underground": "I throw peace to the Bay / cause from the Jungle to Oaktown, they backin' me up all the way."

But no city was large enough to contain the totality of 2Pac's vision. The true target was the United States, and the gold-certified sales of *2Pacalypse Now*—and its attendant controversies—threw the rebel into the machine. His raps were so siren-like that a Texan who shot a public trooper claimed that the album had made him do it. It was soon followed by a blistering condemnation from Vice-punchline Dan Quayle. Compounded by his black-Travis-Bickle turn as Bishop in 1992's *Juice*, Tupac became a bull's-eye before he was old enough legally to cop Old E.

From 1992 until his incarceration in February 1995, Tupac was everywhere. He was in Manhattan hanging out with known thugs like Jimmy Henchman and Haitian Jack and tabloid staples like Madonna and Mickey Rourke. Filming *Above the Rim* and *Poetic Justice* in L.A. Brawling with the Hughes Brothers over a role in *Menace II Society*. After Marin City residents became agitated by his negative portrayal of the projects, he returned home to play the Marin City Festival in August of 1992. A fight broke out and a six-year-old boy was shot in the head by stray bullets. A vengeance-mad mob chased Tupac and his entourage until police arrived to restore order. He only survived by hiding under a parked car. By the time he befriended Biggie the following year, Tupac could already offer weary testament about "mo money, mo problems." (A fan of "Party and Bullshit," Tupac introduced himself to Biggie after watching the latter rock an early show in Maryland.)

A guarded and betrayed 2Pac found his creative energies wandering back to his original coast on 1993's *Strictly 4 My N.I.G.G.A.Z.* Though Shock G and his partners produced "I Get Around" (2Pac's first top-20 hit), his sophomore album largely sought out brimstone East Coast beatmakers like Stretch of Live Squad and Special Ed. Recorded in Richmond, L.A., and New York, *Strictly 4 My N.I.G.G.A.Z.* is 2Pac's purist album: raw, rugged, and with no

A 2Pac Chronology

Joins the 127th Street Repertory Ensemble, in which he plays Travis Younger in *A Raisin in the Sun*. The production is at the Apollo Theater in Harlem.

Joins Digital Underground ("The Humpty Dance") as a dancer and roadie.

First solo album, *2Pacalypse Now,* is released by Interscope Records. Its singles are "Brenda's Got a Baby," "Trapped," and "If My Homie Calls."

Stars in *Poetic Justice* opposite Janet Jackson.

Arrested for allegedly sexually assaulting a woman in a New York hotel room. Tupac is later sentenced to 1½-4½ years in prison and serves for a few months.

1971 | **1983** | **1986** | **1988** | **1990** | **1991** | **November** | **1992** | **January** | **August** | **1993** | **February** | **July** | **November** | **1994** | **September**

Born in East Harlem, New York, to Afeni Shakur and Billy Garland.

Moves to Marin City, California, north of San Francisco.

Juice is released, starring Tupac and Omar Epps. In it Bishop (Tupac) goes on a killing spree.

Strictly 4 My N.I.G.G.A.Z. comes out, debuting at 24 on the Billboard charts.

Moves to Baltimore.

Raps on Digital Underground track "Same Song," from the soundtrack to the movie *Nothing but Trouble* and, subsequently, the DU album *This is an EP Release*.

After a free performance at the Marin City Festival, a fight breaks out. Someone fires a gun, killing a six-year-old boy. Tupac's record company settles a lawsuit following the event, although there was no evidence that Shakur or members of his entourage fired the gun.

Thug Life: Volume 1 comes out, the only album recorded with the group Thug Life (which Tupac had formed along with Big Syke, his stepbrother Mopreme, and others).

Punches director Allen Hughes, whose movie Tupac was set to star in. Spends fifteen days in jail.

Later that month, on November 30, Tupac is robbed of over $35,000 in cash and jewelry and shot five times in the lobby of Quad City Studios. He has to have surgery for a ruptured blood vessel in his leg.

Just one day shy of a year after Tupac began his prison sentence, *All Eyez on Me* is released by Death Row and Interscope. It was the first double album in hip-hop; number 1 on the charts; Rap Album of the Year at the 1997 Soul Train Awards; a groundbreaking achievement on all fronts. The five singles—two of which were number 1 on the Billboard Hot 100—were "How Do U Want It," "California Love," "2 of Amerikaz Most Wanted," "All Bout U," and "I Ain't Mad at Cha."

November 5 *The Don Killuminati: The 7 Day Theory* comes out. It had been recorded in a few days in August. During the first week of its release, the album—released under the pseudonym Makaveli—sells 664,000 copies.

November 1995 | March October 1996 | February September November | 1996-1997

Me Against the World releases a month after Tupac begins his prison sentence at the Clinton Correctional Facility in New York. (It had been recorded earlier.) It debuts at the top spot on the Billboard charts, selling 240,000 copies in its first week. Tracks include "Dear Mama," "So Many Tears," and "Temptations."

During his prison sentence, Tupac marries Keisha Morris, although the marriage is later annulled.

Death Row pays Tupac's $1.4 million bail; he's released from prison.

September 7 Shakur attends a Mike Tyson-Bruce Seldon boxing match at the MGM Grand in Las Vegas. After the match, he is in Suge Knight's BMW when a Cadillac pulls up and starts firing. Tupac is shot four times.

September 13 Tupac Shakur dies of internal bleeding at the University Medical Center in Las Vegas. He is just twenty-five years old.

Tupac is in three films released posthumously: *Bullet* (October 1996), *Gridlock'd* (January 1997; in the *New York Times* Janet Maslin wrote that Tupac has an "appealing mix of presence, confidence and humor"), and *Gang Related* (October 1997). *Gang Related*, which also stars James Earl Jones, is dedicated to Tupac.

Bronze statue (the first ever of a rap star) of Tupac by Tina Allen, at the Tupac Amaru Shakur Center for the Arts in Atlanta. *PR NEWSWIRE / TUPAC AMARU SHAKUR FOUNDATION / AP IMAGES*

frills. Its follow-up, *Me Against the World* (1994), plays almost as a companion piece. Recorded back-to-back at studios on both coasts, *Me Against the World* might be 2Pac's most balanced statement. It fuses the P-Funk bounce of the West with the shrapnel explosions of the post–Bomb Squad East Coast. There's even "Old School," where 2Pac celebrates the early years of New York rap and his own native connection. But mostly, the record bears witness to a time when 2Pac was at his most isolated. He awaited trial for sexual assault on the run; he's a world unto himself, bounded by his barbed-wire scowl and strychnine pen.

You can't ignore the sordid and alienated atmosphere that surrounded the recording of *Me Against the World*. During Biggie and Pac's brief friendship, the former introduced Tupac to a vicious high-living breed of New York hustler. The most infamous was the Queens-bred Haitian Jack, a man so menacing that he intimidated convicted killers.

It was Jack who allegedly convinced Tupac to invite a woman named Ayanna Jackson to his hotel room at New York's Parker Meridien in November of 1993. What occurred in that suite will forever remain nebulous. According to Tupac, Jack, Charles "Man Man" Fuller (Pac's road manager), and an unidentified man interrupted him in flagrante delicto; after Tupac left the room, they allegedly subjected Jackson to forcible sodomy. Jackson insisted that Tupac had lured her in and knew full well what was about to happen. The only thing clear about the incident was that Jack successfully petitioned to separate his case from Shakur's and managed to escape incarceration. In Tupac's eyes, it was a ruthless act of betrayal.

During the same period, Tupac emerged as a folk hero in the South, a development galvanized by an incident in Atlanta in which he shot two white off-duty police officers who had allegedly been harassing an African-American motorist. Pleading self-defense, Tupac beat the charges and cultivated a mythology as a black Bruce Wayne. But even before the Georgia shooting, Tupac had always boasted an early affinity for the region at a time when much of the rap world kept an aloof distance. In a 1992 *Source* feature, he said his favorite album was The Geto Boys' *Grip It! On That Other Level*. Five years later, 2Pac showed further appreciation for the Houston group by rapping on "Smile," the only top-20 single from group member Scarface.

Maybe it was inevitable that Tupac's chameleonic nature found a final cradle in California, the last stand of manifest destiny, a place eternally ready to bleach its roots. After wooing him in jail, Suge Knight posted a $1.4 million bond and brought Tupac home to Death Row's L.A. headquarters. After eight months behind bars, Pac was ripe for reinvention and eager to cloak himself in blood red and wage war on his East Coast enemies. He'd spent extensive time in L.A. before, working on films and brokering a cease-fire between the Bloods and Crips. His lyrics had also frequently memorialized Latasha Harlins, an unarmed South Central teen who had been shot by a Korean storeowner for allegedly shoplifting.

With his number of enemies increasing exponentially with every song and confrontation, death hounded Tupac with a menacing shade. He had become the gangsta rap embodiment of what Joan Didion described as the pioneer experience of crossing nineteenth-century California:

> Each arriving traveler had been, by definition, reborn in the wilderness, a new creature in no way the same as the man . . . who had left Independence or St. Joseph many months before: the very decision to set forth on the journey had been a kind of death, involving the total abandonment of all previous life.

In the land of transplants, 2Pac transformed himself into Makaveli, his own spaghetti Western antihero.

The circumstances of his murder, coupled with an unimpeachable string of classic songs, stamped him as an L.A. icon on par with Magic Johnson (from Michigan), Jack Nicholson (from New Jersey), and Axl Rose (from Mars). The local lyrical ties rest largely on two number-1 singles: "California Love" and "To Live & Die in L.A." The former was famously intended to be Dr. Dre's first single for his new Aftermath imprint, before Suge Knight heard it and allegedly forced him to hand it over to his new star. Its conception of California is as nuanced and effective as a Chamber of Commerce sizzle reel showing glistening ocean and golden sunshine to a Clevelander in the dead of December. Except that 2Pac's civic boosterism comes with an ominous caveat: "Caution, we collide with other crews."

His Death Row masterpieces, *All Eyez on Me* and *The Don Killuminati: The 7 Day Theory*, are pure gangsta music, invective as ammunition, syllables with enough artillery for decades. But even though 2Pac never stopped making music for the hood, he crossed over to the point where you will still hear "Ambitionz Az A Ridah" blaring out of the Beamers of Persian kids in Beverly Hills. At Coachella in 2012, a 2Pac hologram roared "Hail Mary" and unified a crowd young enough to have been conceived to a new cassette

THE HOLOPAC

There are moments when you realize that you are living in the future: when you realize that filling up your gas tank costs as much as the rent of a beachfront Venice apartment in the Jim Morrison era; when you realize that your pocket-sized smart phone can instantly summon more information than the ancient library of Alexandria; when you go to a rock festival and see a hologram performance by a rapper who has been dead since the start of Clinton's second term.

2Pac performed at Coachella 2012 alongside Snoop Dogg and Dr. Dre. He was still shirtless and still sporting the same tattoos and 2 percent body fat, despite not having been to a Bally's Fitness in almost twenty years. He rapped every word to "Hail Mary" and yelled "What's up, Coachella?" before a crowd of kids who were in kindergarten when he got capped. I was there. It was weird and discomfiting, but it received a bigger roar than any other artist that weekend, including Radiohead and Pac's still-living Death Row label mates.

It was a *Chappelle's Show* skit come to life, except that no one wanted to pretend that he wasn't alive. It was tasteful, ridiculous, cheesy, and totally fitting. The myth of 2Pac has metastasized so much that a hologram image was

Tupac hologram at Coachella, 2012. *PHOTO BY KEVIN WINTER / GETTY IMAGES*

"HoloPac" and Snoop. *PHOTO BY CHRISTOPHER POLK / GETTY IMAGES*

scarcely less realistic than the ideas of him that we have in
our heads.

James Cameron's visual production firm, Digital Domain, and
two hologram-imaging companies, AV Concepts and Musion Systems,
were to blame for the incorporeal 2Pac. How fitting that the
man behind *The Terminator* was partially behind the concept of
reviving a man whose ferocity was Schwarzeneggerian.

Despite the Disneyland *Haunted Mansion* effects, the
HoloPac was well received. There was talk of tour plans and
resuscitating other deceased celebrities. A fake Hologram
Tupac Twitter immediately racked up twenty-six thousand Twitter
followers. But the schemes never materialized and less than six
months after Coachella, Digital Domain filed for bankruptcy.
You can almost hear 2Pac taunting them: keep your mind on your
money and your money on your mind.

tape of *2Pacalypse Now*. In Southern California, he has become Walt Disney for those down to ride.

If Biggie reflected the literary tradition of New York, 2Pac's vision of Los Angeles is blockbuster and cinematic. "To Live & Die in L.A." offers a happy ending, a scripted antidote to the reputation for sunshine dystopia that L.A. had acquired in the wake of the Rodney King riots. The city is brought together by its shared hustle, the desire to flock to the end of the earth in search of economic opportunity, and the possibility of eradicating the past. After all, the name "To Live & Die in L.A." was shared by a 1985 film described by *Variety* as a "rich man's Miami Vice," with a soundtrack scored by Wang Chung.

2Pac understood how to flatter, shouting out Mexicans, Sunset Blvd., South Central, Crenshaw, MLK Blvd., mom and pop record stores, the local

Street Soldier, **by Steven Braunstein. Digital illustration, 2012.** COURTESY OF THE ARTIST

rap radio stations, and even A&Rs (the talent divisions for record labels). Yet as in nearly every story ever written about Los Angeles, an uneasy undercurrent of noir exists. 2Pac sheds tears at a burial of a close friend, maligns Pete Wilson's conservative governance, and worries about the court cases looming over his head.

In a constantly mutating metropolis afflicted by an amnesia toward its real and imagined past, 2Pac understood that most would really only remember the hook's last words: "To Live & Die in L.A., it's the place to be. You've got to be there to know it, everybody wanna see."

It's a pat on the back, the idea that the finish line was crossed at the city limits; victory was merely a matter of making it to the golden land. After all, every city needs something to play at parades.

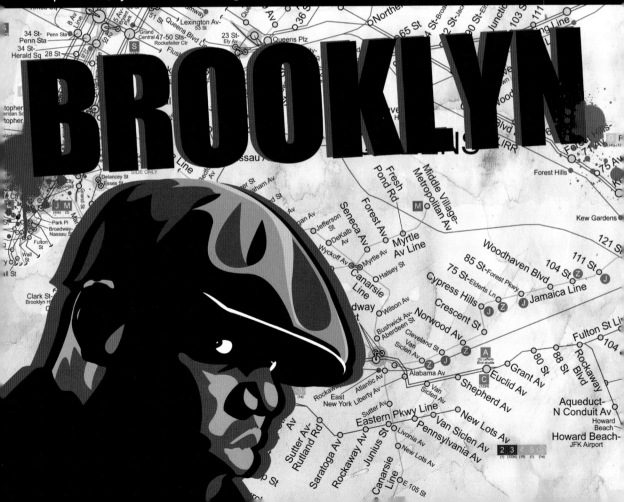

Spread Love, by Steven Braunstein. Digital illustration, 2012. *COURTESY OF THE ARTIST*

BIGGIE

When the poet Hart Crane describes the social and spiritual zone of New York in 1930's "The Bridge," he begins with one particular tendon of the city: The Brooklyn Bridge. In the opening section, "To Brooklyn Bridge," Crane's speaker offers the colossal span of concrete and steel as a new kind of religious site, a place where New Yorkers arrive for an experience simultaneously personal and communal. It becomes the unchanging cathedral, the "harp and altar, of the fury fused." It endures while the masses sit inside movie theaters and watch "panoramic sleights / With multitudes bent toward some flashing scene / Never disclosed, but hastened to again, / Foretold to other eyes on the same screen."

New York gains its inimitable power through this tension between icon and crowd. New York is a city of landmarks compressed together: Chrysler Building, Empire State Building, Central Park, Grand Army Plaza, World's Fair Unisphere in Corona Park, Statue of Liberty, Union Square, Co-Op City, Bronx Botanical Gardens, Grand Central Station, Federal Hall, St. Patrick's Cathedral, Williamsburg Bridge, George Washington Bridge, Brooklyn Bridge. You get the idea.

And yet New York splinters into borough-specific regionalism. Christopher Wallace came of age during the years when Queens' Juice Crew and the Bronx's Boogie Down Productions waged their musical war over the true birthplace of hip-hop. The Juice Crew's "The Bridge" (1986) begat Boogie Down's "South Bronx," which begat KRS-One's rise to hip-hop superstardom. BDP and the Bronx won that genesis-centered debate, but the neighborhood anthems of the 1980s went beyond the so-called Bridge Wars. Minor releases like the Divine Sounds' "Do Or Die Bed Stuy" in 1984 and 1989's "The Bush" from Special Ed planted flags for Brooklyn (see 2011's

"Ten Great Neighborhood-Specific Brooklyn Rap Anthems" in the *Village Voice* for even more examples). These sectarian anthems made the pressure between block-by-block neighborhood and sprawling metropolis real.

By the time Biggie began recording music beneath Fulton Street in the early 1990s, there was already a mantle of responsibility for young New York MCs: represent your neighborhood while simultaneously representing New York City. Speak to the masses gazing at the bridge and the individual moviegoer living his own personal fantasy. Biggie's strategy here was at the very core of his musical accomplishment and at the very core of what made him a quintessential New York artist. He embodied the zeitgeist and mood of his city by creating a simultaneously public and private New York. These contradicting impulses imbue his music with the specific/universal tension that all great art has to contain. Biggie created an eternal neighborhood chant—"Where Brooklyn at!?"—in a 1993 freestyle you can find remixed

Brooklyn Bridge. *PETER D. / SHUTTERSTOCK.COM*

and collected in his posthumous *Born Again*, and yet he recorded no borough-centric anthem. His thirst for material culture and balance of humor and horror seem completely Gothamite, and yet his most vivid song about being a New Yorker is about being a New Yorker appreciating life outside New York: "Goin' Back To Cali." Whereas Biggie is unflinching in his reportage about life in the cocaine business—he literally bills "Ten Crack Commandments" as a "manual"—he gives only glimpses of his life in the trade. He mentions a court case here, a mayor there.

So, in the end, what makes Biggie so inexorably tied to New York? Biggie's and the city's obsessions are the same: work, compression, instruction, material culture, and juxtaposition. To listen to a Biggie song is to engage in conversation with a real New Yorker: someone who will break up his lecture by pointing to a storefront or passerby, someone who offers splinters of history in the midst of his daily toil. Where, to this listener, 2Pac is almost exclusively a lyrical MC, Biggie oscillates between narrative action and lyrical reflection in the same song. He's a New Yorker because he has to be in one thousand places at once.

"Everyday Struggle" from *Ready To Die* emblemizes this frantic compression. At first a lyrical reflection of rising in the crack game, Biggie slips in slivers of historical/geographic reference. The song opens generally: "I know how it feel to wake up fucked up / Pockets broke as hell, another rock to sell / People look at you like you's the user / Selling drugs to all the losers, mad buddha abuser." The link between dealer and user, the crushing grind of the drug trade—although not quite so general as to be hustler platitudes, these lines are hardly exact. However, that "people" in the third bar speaks to something bustling, something metropolitan. The "people" going about their business in Brooklyn would see Biggie's speaker selling on the corner. Hustlers in small towns have out-of-the-way corners and streets to themselves. In bustling Bed-Stuy? No such luck.

Then, in the second half of the first verse and the entirety of the second, Biggie begins to divulge more to the listener. You imagine him wrapping his arm around you, revealing perhaps a bit too much in his percussive rendering of detail. In that first verse, he tells us that his mother kicked him out once "I figured out that nic's went for twenty down south." This lone line supplies an explicit nod to his pre–Bad Boy stint as a dealer in North Carolina, in which, according to interviews, he could sell crack for four times the price he could in New York. New York, the center, the metropolis, provides the material product that the periphery, the comparative sticks of North Carolina, will pay top dollar for. Biggie, the New Yorker, has to go on a business trip to sell his wares. That verse ends with New York, if not the city proper, pulling him back, "Smokin' mad Newports cause I'm due in court / for an assault that I caught in Bridgeport, New York." He has to specify "New York" after Bridgeport not just because it fills out the rhyme scheme, but because any real New Yorker would assume that Bridgeport refers to the poor former industrial town in Connecticut an hour's drive up 95.

The verse becomes more specific as it proceeds. The details become fixed to Biggie's work life. He starts talking about his daughter and his

The Meadowlands, New Jersey, 1995.
PHOTO BY DAVID CORIO / GETTY IMAGES

A Notorious B.I.G. Chronology

Appears in "Unsigned Hype" column in *Source*. Meets Sean Combs later that year.

Bad Boy Records releases Biggie's debut, Ready To Die, with the lead single "Juicy."

Returns to Brooklyn. Records first demos with DJ 50 Grand and Old Gold Brothers crew.

They marry.

Ready To Die goes platinum—1 million copies sold.

Drops out of Westinghouse High School.

Wallace meets Faith Evans at a photo shoot.

1972 ▎ 1989 ▎ 1990 ▎ 1992 ▎ March ▎ 1993 ▎ August ▎ 1994 ▎ June ▎ August ▎ September ▎ November ▎ 1995 ▎ January ▎ March

Born in Brooklyn, New York, to Voletta Wallace and George Letore.

After appearing on a few posse cuts (as Biggie Smalls) and providing the rap verse on the remix to Mary J. Blige's "Real Love," gets his first solo single, "Party and Bullshit," the first song and single off the soundtrack to the Ted Demme comedy *Who's The Man?* Sean Combs, the Uptown Records A&R man who signed him, is fired. He founds Bad Boy Records.

The RIAA certifies *Ready To Die* gold—half a million copies sold.

Shakur gives an interview to Kevin Powell of *Vibe* during which he tells the story of his shooting in New York. He implicates Combs and Wallace in his shooting.

Wallace, according to interviews, lives in Raleigh, North Carolina, full-time to traffic crack cocaine.

Tupac Shakur is robbed and shot in the basement of a Manhattan recording studio where Wallace records with Combs.

Wallace's daughter T'yanna is born.

Life After Death recording sessions begin during the fall. Wallace records new songs, according to Coker, "at a breakneck pace."

Combs and Wallace are satirized (as "P.I.G." and "Buffy") in Shakur's music video for "2 of Americaz Most Wanted."

Wallace and Combs film the music video for *Life After Death*'s lead single, "Hypnotize," in Los Angeles. They remain in L.A.

The *New York Times Magazine* publishes a feature on Death Row. In it, Suge Knight and Tupac insinuate that Shakur has had sex with Evans.

October 30
Evans gives birth to Christopher Wallace Jr.

| August | **1996** | January | March | May | September | October | **1997** | February | March |

Wallace performs with other Bad Boy artists at the Source Awards in New York City. He wins multiple awards, including Best New Artist and Album of the Year. Also in August, Junior M.A.F.I.A.'s debut album, *Conspiracy*, is released. Wallace is a co-executive producer and supplies guest verses for the singles "Get Money" and "Player's Anthem."

Wallace, Combs, Knight, and Shakur have a brief, tense interaction at the Soul Train Awards in Los Angeles.

September 7
Tupac Shakur is shot in Las Vegas after attending a Mike Tyson fight.

September 13
Tupac dies in the hospital.

September 17
Wallace is in a near-fatal accident in New Jersey. Leg shattered, he will require a cane for the rest of his life.

Night of March 8/morning of March 9
Wallace is shot and killed after attending an after-party for the 1997 Soul Train Awards.

March 25
Life After death is released. Album goes on to receive the RIAA's "Diamond" certification for over 10 million records sold.

morning stress. He ends the verse by complaining about his job and all the places that aren't the big city. For anyone who is or has been a New Yorker, or even knows one, this verbal tactic should sound awfully familiar.

The second verse opens outside New York too. Here Biggie thrusts the listener immediately into a drug narrative:

> I had the master plan, I'm in the caravan on the way to Maryland
> With my man Two-Tecs to take over this projects
> They call him Two-Tecs, he tote two tecs
> And when he start to bust, he like to ask, "Who's next?"
> I got my honey on the Amtrak with the crack
> In the crack of her ass, two pounds of hash in the stash.

Biggie smashes two simultaneous stories together. He's leaving New York with an accomplice at the same time that his underling mules leave on the train. This is modern metropolitan action. Biggie enacts it by leaping immediately from (the fictional) Two-Tecs' question to the next slice of life. Like the Brooklyn Bridge of Hart Crane's poetry, Biggie's specific details anchor the imagined narratives. He stacks his images into a metropolitan verticality. There's never just one thing happening in a Biggie song; a great chain of events spirals up from every line and down from every image.

Biggie creates his New York through a cornucopia of small details. (If he has a central image like Crane's bridge, it's crack cocaine.) Like that list of New York landmarks that speak to the tourist, Biggie pulls the generalities of the hustler's life into diamond-cut relief through details that act as pivots between the narrative and the lyric. He lets the details compress narratives that could, in the hands of a less urgent MC, spiral into redundancy. Where 2Pac lingers with figures—his mother, a former foe—and gives them entire songs in which he praises, rages, and reflects, Biggie sketches a whole character in a line. He summons a cultural moment with a reference.

The final verse of "Everyday Struggle" opens with references to two omnipresent and seemingly omnipotent figures of 1990s New York: "I'm seeing body after body and our Mayor Giuliani / ain't tryin' to see no black man turn to John Gotti." This couplet lays a new set of New York–specific tensions. La Costa Nostra—the Italian mob—became the iconic model around which mid-to-late 1990s so-called Mafioso rap (Wu Tang Clan's Raekwon, Puff Daddy's *No Way Out, Life After Death*) built its personalities.

John Gotti, who unabashedly sold narcotics at a time when many old-guard members of the mob still saw the trade as forbidden, who ordered the legendary hit on Gambino family elders outside Sparks Steak House in Midtown, is one model of absolute power. And Rudy Giuliani, who transformed himself from a lisping, opportunistic, party-swapping narcotics prosecutor to a mayor, who imprisoned young black men for jumping subway turnstiles and breaking windows, acts as the other. These two nodes of achievement, the Teflon Don and Rudy, had hustled their way to the heights of criminal and political power, respectively.

The choice of one ladder versus the other clearly spoke to Biggie's own choices. The drug trade offered more immediate riches, and Biggie knew he could succeed in the field. But he was catching fire in the above-ground, taxable future of the rap game. By 1992, Biggie had already appeared in *The Source* magazine's "Unsigned Hype" column, and yet he still trafficked weight. It would be one side of the bridge or another for Christopher Wallace. The conflation of those two sides—the legitimate and the not—

The Institute of Higher Burnin', or 5Pointz, an outdoor art exhibit in Long Island City, New York. 2010. © FREDERIC SOLTAN / CORBIS

makes the final verse of "Everyday Struggle" resonate with a cosmopolitan urgency: where in this city do you want to go? Which landmarks do you wish to make your own? Which fantasy will you make real?

Unlike 2Pac—whose vagabond life and rambling experience through America gave him the material to make spiritual, universal lyrics—Biggie's own life was built around New York. (Yes, his time in North Carolina as a dealer was formative. According to Coker's interview with Biggie's former associate Robert Cagle in *Notorious*, it was at a Days Inn during a 1990 run to North Carolina that the two of them watched the 1975 caper flick *Let's Do It Again*, starring Sidney Poitier and Bill Cosby. The film had a character named Biggie Smalls; Cagle suggested that Wallace, then going simply by "Biggie," add "Smalls" to his nom de plume for some levity. Wallace agreed.) But the rich, almost overflowing hip-hop scene in 1990s New York meant that Biggie, if he were to become the MC that he and others knew he could be, would have to commit to making one fantasy real. It meant representing Bed-Stuy—Biggie's most frequent geographic tactic is either to open a verse by locating himself as a son of Bed-Stuy or to turn to the reference mid-verse—while rapping about broader metropolitan tropes.

What makes Biggie a New York artist at the most essential level is his sense of combination. It was impossible for him to record a one-note song: his love songs involve crime and loss; his crime songs involve benign childhood anecdotes; he would throw five micro-narratives into a song when a lesser artist would struggle to manage one.

In his brilliantly apocalyptic book on New York architecture, *Delirious New York*, Rem Koolhaas argues that the recursive grid structure of New York required builders to "develop a new system of formal values, to invest strategies for the distinction of one block from another. . . . The Grid defines a new balance between control and de-control in which the city can be at the same time ordered and fluid, a metropolis of rigid chaos." I cannot invent a better metaphor for Biggie's own work. It exists on this grid of public reference and symbol. It thrives on the line between general sentiment (work is rough; parenting transforms) and surreal symbol (guys named Two-Tecs). Biggie's words evoke that grid that contains narrative sequence and lyric ornament, public spectacle and private ritual. His words are immigrants, remaking themselves against the churning forces of New York City.

Chapter 3

AESTHETIC APPEARANCES & EXPERIENCES

2PAC

It takes a special sort of man to wear leather. For instance, you or I should not wear leather. I'm not talking about the brown leather jacket you bought at Banana Republic to match your chinos.

I'm not talking about a *City Slickers*–ready pair of boots. I'm talking *leather*. Hells Angels leather. Jim Morrison leather. *Wild One* leather. 2Pac leather.

There is a thin line between leather and outright insanity. It's the last fashion bastion before you drape yourselves in feathers, leaves, and Oglala Sioux war paint.

The wrong leather and you're immediately fast-tracked to a Germanic goth sex palace. When was the last time you saw a shirtless man walking down the street in a skintight black leather vest with zippers on the front? What did you think? Exactly. But that was what 2Pac wore on the cover of *All Eyez on Me*—with the words *Safe Sex* inscribed on the left breast. And the world almost unanimously agreed that he was absolutely terrifying, a rap Thor. This is power . . . or something.

His tattoos tell the tale. Start with the chest. His first tattoo: the word *2Pac*. Make no mistake, Tupac and 2Pac were different creatures. Examine any creation myth or Joseph Campbell journey. This was his warrior's path—the rap game—a way to sate his wandering creativity, lust for fame, and empty stomach. The tattoos were figurative war wounds that soon matched literal scars. 2Pac was dedicated to deliquescing the memory of the bookish boy-in-the-corner, picked on for any number of trivial flaws. 2Pac was psychologically barricaded to absorb all bullets and spit them back at exponential velocity.

Mid-torso: a machine gun emblazoned with the words *50 Niggaz*. Converted into 2Pac's slanguage, the acronym stood for "Never Ignorant, Getting Goals Accomplished." Even his body was an attempt to reclaim words, code them in familiar symbols, and stake his own flags.

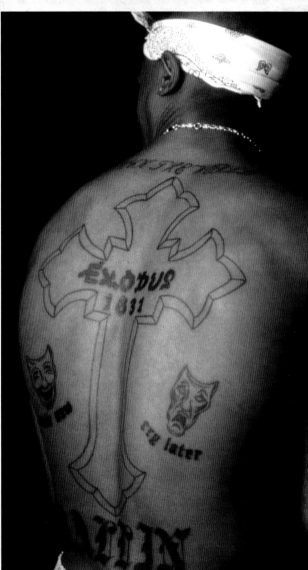

© CHI MODU, DIVERSE IMAGES / CORBIS

To the right is a bust of Queen Nefertiti, the wife of the Egyptian pharaoh Akhenaten. Together the royals had ushered in the worship of Aten, the sun god. Beneath her face read the words *2 Die 4*. One of the most powerful women of ancient African lore, it's unquestionable that 2Pac saw her as a synecdoche for all black women. I don't need to tell you that 2Pac was capable of misogyny. "All Bout U" does a good enough job (with great Million Man March gags). But no matter how extreme he got, he rarely forgot his mother and sister's plight. The tattoo was another reminder, a silent memorial to the trauma he'd seen them endure. His lyrics flesh out the picture. Whenever 2Pac talks about his "black queens," it is Nefertiti he's describing, it is Afeni, it is any woman who ever offered him physical or emotional harbor.

Straight down his spine was a massive block-script crucifix with the biblical marking Exodus, 18:31, which states: "Now I know that the Lord is greater than all Gods because he delivered the people from the hands of the Egyptians when they dealt with them arrogantly." It encapsulates his attitude and turbulent spirituality as neatly as anything. He is the modern vessel for the rebellious spirit. He believes a higher reward will come for those born to resist. He identifies with the runaway slave, parting seas and shattering empires. This is the legacy of his namesake.

On his left lat is the jolly mask of Greek drama, "Laugh Now." Its tragic partner, "Cry Later," adorns his right side. Not only is it a direct reference to his thespian roots, it's a nod toward the separate spheres of his personality. The Tupac who emerged from prison was loose-wired and enraged. He had seen good times corrode into ambulance trips. He was a man acutely aware of his mortality and the consequences of his actions. His response to the existential void was answered on the tattoo just below: *B A L L I N*.

Everybody wants to ball. The slang word is versatile enough. It can mean hoop, fuck, or wild out. It alludes to both living in the moment and riding out on all the suckers. Tupac belonged to a special class of baller. Everyone from Jasmine Guy and Madonna to Haitian Jack and Jimmy Henchman wanted to kick it with him. Re-examine that same cover of *All Eyez on Me*. He is smoking on a boat sipping what appears to be a banana daiquiri (maybe Thug Passion, aka champagne and Alizé, Tupac's drink of choice?). Money looks limitless. He is young, black, and gifted. Tupac may not have invented ballin, but he perfected it. And he could sell that to you with the raise of a glass and the lift of an eyebrow.

Finery at the 1996 MTV Video Music Awards (Snoop and Tupac presented Best Hard Rock Video). *PHOTO BY KEVIN MAZUR / WIREIMAGE / GETTY IMAGES*

Biceps, forearms, shoulders, neck: a panther head; Jesus' head on a burning cross; a skull and crossbones; the words *heartless, playaz, Westside, outlaw, notorious, Makaveli,* and *mob;* the phrases *trust no one, fuck the world, Only God Can Judge Me,* and *my only fear of death is coming back reincarnated.* He was a Hells Angel in rap form—the bandit in all black in a 500 Benz balling toward Gehenna.

The coup d'état was *Thug Life* across his abdomen. Like Christ and all his rock star disciples, Tupac had the chiseled physique fit to be plastered on a hundred million stucco walls. *Thug Life* was mantra—particularly when Tupac flipped it into the acronym "The Hate U Give Lil Infants Fuck Everybody." *Thug Life* became the war cry that he and his fans used to inflict revenge on their enemies. He had sublimated and spit back Dr. Johnson's maxim about becoming a beast to erase the pain of being a man.

That's why Tupac could wear leather. His frame was temple to his invincibility: scars and long eyelashes, hedonism and its hellish rewards immolating in a 5-foot-9, 165-pound fireball. So every girl still swoons at him the way they still revere James Dean or Kurt Cobain. His early death forever enshrouded him in that pantheon of outlaw sex symbols, the only black man crashing the *Rolling Stone*–thrown wine and weed party.

This is the iconic image of Tupac, not the original impression. The world first peeped 2Pac in the 1991 video for Digital Underground's "Same Song." How better to introduce new rap royalty than by having him ushered in on a king carrier surrounded by solemn thugs in dashikis? Wearing a crown—a pointed banana-shaded kufi—and dozens of African chains and clutching a staff, 2Pac looked like the hip-hop incarnation of *Coming to America's* Prince Akeem.

In 1991, one year prior to Dre's *The Chronic,* 2Pac's Black Panther bonafides fit snugly into the clenched fists and brimstone rhetoric of the Afrocentric era. But rap fashion and slang move at a runway-world velocity. Several months later, 2Pac blew up with the "Brenda's Got a Baby" video. By now, he had a deal on fledgling Interscope Records, and his ripped-from-the-headlines eulogy to a slain prostitute named Brenda earned heavy rotation on *Yo! MTV Raps.* Stark black-and-white visuals replaced the camp of "Same Song." 2Pac wears a beanie, baggie jeans, and thick parka. A diamond stud glints in his nose. The piercing became one of his most distinctive visual characteristics, a mark of androgyny that softened his coarse aggression.

RECIPE FOR THUG PASSION

2 oz. champagne, 2 oz. Alizé.

Or an alternative can be found at the Stark Bar at the Los
Angeles County Museum of Art:
2Pactail ($14)
Blanche Armagnac, local raspberries, fresh lemon juice,
champagne.

By album number two, 2Pac was shirtless on the cover. LL Cool J and Big Daddy Kane may have been the rap game's Alfred Kinseys for introducing sexualization to marketing schemes, but 2Pac rewrote the report. This was no accident. The mainstreaming of the genre started in the early 1990s, with female listeners playing an increasingly important role in its popularization. 2Pac understood this from jump, famously telling Biggie, "You gotta rap for the bitches." You had to dress for them too. He was both the bathing suit–clad mack in "I Get Around" and the Thinker in a black jean jacket on the cover of *Me Against the World*. In his own way, he might have been the 1990s gangsta rap parallel to Dylan McKay (the *Beverly Hills 90210* teen soap stand-in for James Dean). Same familiar archetype: bad-boy rebels from

Tampa, Florida, mural, 2011.
© EDMUND D. FOUNTAIN / ZUMA PRESS / CORBIS

broken homes, closet intellectuals, unusually sensitive, eager to fight. In this scenario, Steve Sanders is played by Snoop Dogg.

At the 1994 Source Awards, Tupac is at the height of thug life. Beleaguered by legal and financial stress, he's at his most sartorially modest: a backwards baseball cap, red sweatshirt, and a single silver crucifix. Shortly thereafter, he swapped the blood colors for prison blues, a muting that inevitably led to the flamboyant reaction of his final Death Row years.

Flamboyant seems too timid an adjective to describe the 1995 "California Love" video. Out on bail, fresh out of jail, 2Pac, Dr. Dre, and Hype Williams created a post-apocalyptic Golden State in which Oakland was overrun by fire, steel cages, girls in leather miniskirts, and men dressed like Mad Max by way of the Legion of Doom. Also included in the census: Funk master Roger Troutman, Chris Tucker, and the dwarf from *Bad Santa*. Biggie had morphed from Big Poppa into the King of New York, but 2Pac had seen the future. And the future had bandannas, tunics, and leather.

There is another "California Love" video, but no one remembers it. Intended to be the sequel, 2Pac wakes up from his Thunderdome dream and calls up Dre to shop at the Compton Swap Meet. Then they party with Deion Sanders, DJ Quik, and E-40. This was probably a more realistic approximation of their real lives, but realism matters less than believability. I am much more inclined to believe that 2Pac inhabited a bizarro 2095 Bay Area than a place where he and Dre went shopping for Jerry Stackhouse Fila's at the Compton Swap Meet.

The flipside was 2Pac as elegant don. Biggie limped, prematurely aged like Marlon Brando as Don Corleone, wearing heavy linen suits that seemed to match the disproportionate weights on his mind and frame. My co-author Evan may claim that Biggie was Michael Corleone, but to me, 2Pac has always been Michael, swaggering and deadly, a primal manifestation of youth. See him in the video for "2 of Amerikaz Most Wanted," the baby-faced gangster floating in the black Benz, casually smoking, feasting, threatening. Or examine his appearance at the 1996 Grammys, clad in an all-black Versace suit, no tie, Death Row chain swinging. He smirks and tells the crowd: "How you like this Versace hook-up, the swap meet was closed." He knows how far he's come from the kid with $5 in his pocket, Greyhounding it all the way to Oakland. Vowing to enliven the staid Grammys, he then introduces Kiss.

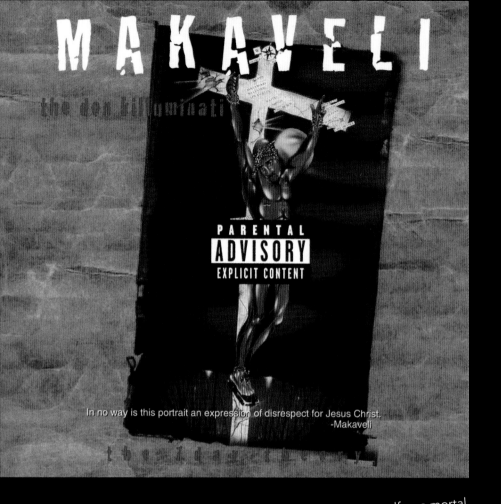

MAKAVELI

the don killuminati

PARENTAL
ADVISORY
EXPLICIT CONTENT

In no way is this portrait an expression of disrespect for Jesus Christ.
-Makaveli

You know how this story winds up. When you frame yourself as a mortal deity, martyrdom is the only possible end result. Tupac may not have been alive to offer input on *The Don Killuminati: The 7 Day Theory* album cover, but it may be his most haunting image. Pac in the bandanna, shirtless, nailed dead to a cross. Biggie created a stylish gangster flick with an eye for detail that Coppola might envy. But Pac was already a movie star. So he wrote his own leather-bound mythology that became posthumous religion.

(Following pages) *Dead Poets*, by Clay O'Brien, 2011. "Both 2Pac and B.I.G. are behind a half wall riddled with bullet holes, yet they remain stone-faced and determined. Both have found a way to live forever . . . through their music and their message." —O'Brien COURTESY OF THE ARTIST, THE CLAY O'BRIEN ART CO. WWW.THECOACO.COM

BIGGIE

The tragedy of The Notorious B.I.G.'s short life provides a clear division of style: early Biggie and late Biggie. The pyrotechnic fury of early Biggie's voice—each word drips with desire— becomes the guttural, lumbering tremor of his *Life After Death*– era recordings, when he weighed nearly four hundred pounds and relied on a cane to walk (after a 1996 car accident). The unlaced Tim's and XXXL T-shirts give way to taupe three-piece suits, fedoras, and vintage sunglasses. The lashing street corner freestyles become his imperial, domineering performance at the 1995 Source Awards. What remained constant was the colossal scope of Biggie, the bottomless pit of sound and hunger.

Chocolate milk. Pickle juice. Mad blunts. Gin. Cracked crab. Lobster. Coogi sweaters. MAC-10s. Private Stock. Bacardi Dark. Sex in expensive cars. Whether he's The Notorious B.I.G. or Biggie Smalls or Christopher Wallace or the Black Frank White (taken from the titular Christopher Walken role in *King of New York*), we speak of a man driven by appetites. The ceaseless appetites make the presence. And Biggie's presence devoured the space around him.

You can hear the burgeoning baritone in his first single, 1993's "Party and Bullshit." He raps with an adolescent hunger: "Conversation, blunts in rotation / My man Big Jacques got the Glock in the waist / and we're smoking, drinking, got the hooker thinking / If money smell bad then this nigga Biggie stinkin'." There's no differentiation between the chatter, the weed, the girls, the drink, and the violence. It's all happening at once. Biggie's hunger is universal. Destructive appetitive constructs his identity. He's hungry for a scene, for an atmosphere. Biggie renders tangible aspects of the scene without any explicit detail—but that's kind of the point. Rare is the nineteen-year-old who particularly cares what exactly he drinks and eats and screws. As long as those things are all happening, he's good.

Biggie's voice snaps in "Party and Bullshit." The young Biggie doesn't so much warp conventional stresses as he chews them. He grunts the taut, tiny *i* sounds in "thinkin'" and "stinkin'."

PHOTO BY CHRIS WALTER / WIREIMAGE / GETTY IMAGES

"I see you shivering / Check the flavor Biggie Smalls is delivering / Lyrical lyricist flowing lyrics out my larynx." — "Dolly My Baby (Bad Boy Remix)"

He cranks his voice up to a roar in the rounded open mouth vowels, *ai's* and *ee's* and *o's*. When he says "Heineken" later in the song, he turns the natural first syllable stress into a blasting cap and lets the small *e* sound in *ken* land with a thud.

These are the aesthetic choices of a young artist. Early 1990s Biggie raps with metrical rigor. It's a choice that many a young poet or jazz musician has made. Because all of Biggie's songs engage with the

Circa 1997. *PHOTOFEST*

theme of craft—whether slinging or rapping—the choice sounds doubly natural. He pops the first and last syllables of lines, flicking emphasis on and off to give each verse a percussive, deliberate energy. He never abandoned this technique fully, but listening to the later recordings, one hears more moments of conversation, of vivid speech. But on "Party and Bullshit" and in the furious metrical peaks of *Ready To Die*—"Machine Gun Funk," "Respect," and "Unbelievable"—the astonishingly agile flow turns verses into cascades.

The images of early-career Biggie contain key details of this apprentice aura. Even though 2Pac's attitude changed from that of a backup dancer to revolutionary thug poet, his appearance remained relatively constant—as

Jeff pointed out, he and Jim Morrison are the two preeminent icons for the shirtless, lithe seeker. In contrast, Biggie let his dress craft his identity. The barebones wardrobe of boots, billowing T-shirt, blue denim, and black down jacket match his perturbed 1992 baby face. He's in uniform. The uniform is a hustler's—a hustler with cherubic features he's worked into a baby-faced scowl, but a hustler all the same.

Desire stems from absence. The young dealer feels stark in the functionality of boots and jeans and a T-shirt. The infant on the cover of *Ready To Die* sits on a white field with nothing on his body but a diaper. Surely this child is not ready to die in the way that old men are ready to die, having made peace with the earth and their families. The child is ready to die *for something*—for material success, for a legacy, for work, for the future security of a family. For something. 2Pac's songs reflect the desire for spiritual knowledge and the desire to impart that knowledge to an audience. Biggie's fleshy, tangible sense of life and purpose is rooted in a physical desire. 2Pac's songs speak to the heart; Biggie's to the senses. On "Juicy," the fusion of deep emotion and tangible proof is transparent: he pledges fatherhood to his daughter by promising to put diamonds in her ears.

To himself, he pledges physical transformation. The evolution in Biggie's visual presence mirrors the transformation we hope for in ourselves. We want to upgrade from hoodies to suits. We want to move from zealously proving our work's worth to receiving praise for nonchalant excellence. The cover

1995, outside Biggie's mother's house (with Junior M.A.F.I.A.).
PHOTOGRAPH BY CLARENCE DAVIS / NY DAILY NEWS VIA GETTY IMAGES

Biggie and Puffy: the faces of Bad Boy.

of his first album: a diapered baby with an Afro. The cover of his second: a bowed, colossal kingpin in a three-piece suit, leaning on a cane, peeking out from the side of a hearse. Even in his photos, Biggie embodies the concept of compression. He runs through the Shakespearean seven stages of man, from infancy to old age and death, in barely a half-decade of photographs, videos, and songs. He chronicles schoolboy aspirations through clothes like his self-made Lacostes in "Sky's The Limit." In "You're Nobody (Til Somebody Kills You)" a precociously aged Biggie elegizes himself in the third person and through more luxury: "Remember he used to push the champagne Range?"

At the 1995 Source Awards in New York, the East Coast–West Coast animus dominated the show as it dominated contemporary hip-hop. The Bad Boy family was the centerpiece of the show. Junior M.A.F.I.A., Bad Boy's ostensible crew, had just released *Conspiracy*, their debut. The then-Puff Daddy, Sean Combs, had become the Tom Hagen to Big's Michael Corleone. Biggie's own *Ready To Die* was a year old and was already regarded as a canonical East Coast hardcore album.

The Bad Boy performance recalled the classic smorgasbord style of Motown shows. After Craig Mack's "Flava In Ya Year" came Faith Evans. After Evans, Biggie stepped on stage for a few rhymes before the girl group Total arrived to sing "Can't You See." Biggie reclined in a literal throne stage right. He rose for Junior M.A.F.I.A.'s "Player's Anthem" as a half-dozen white-towel-waving anonymous hypemen took the stage. Everyone Bad Boy wore black.

Obviously Biggie was the center of the performance. While never spritely, he moved on stage authoritatively, pacing in front of backup dancers while Puffy dipped, shouted, and swiveled around him. At the end of the performance, when Lil' Kim clomped to the stage's front in a black cocktail dress, Biggie glided around to stage left. Like a creative genius around which a corporate body is built, Biggie was flanked by reflections of himself. (The scene recalls the end of the first *Godfather*, when Michael receives his capos in his office, his first act as Don.)

It was an odd sight. Christopher Wallace, an only child who quite literally loomed larger than his childhood peers, an MC whose debut made room for only one guest verse, seemed to have spent so much of the first movements of his life, by choice or not, alone. In his Source Awards performance he had subordinates, a partner, and a crowd hanging onto every syllable. He appeared sated. As the froth of rap sectarianism and Suge Knight vs. Puffy brinkmanship swirled around him, and the friendship between him and 2Pac petrified into venomous mistrust, The Notorious B.I.G. was nearly stationary. His lines sprayed verve. His right hand tilted the mic toward his mouth, and his left chopped the air in front of his face. His body turned and bent slightly like a tall, mature tree leaning in strong wind.

The next two years pressurized the atmosphere around him. The conflict between East Coast and West Coast hip-hop filled the airwaves. The apex of hip-hop was an unenviable place to rest in the 1990s. Truly excellent albums were released at an ungodly clip. A generation of MCs found its voice and best-fit style simultaneously. New albums expanded and deepened the fatalism (Mobb Deep's *The Infamous*), the linguistic energy (GZA's *Liquid Swords*), and the coming-of-age scope (Jay-Z's *Reasonable Doubt*) that made *Ready To Die* such an excellent debut. The music video was replacing the freestyle and demo tapes as the cultural coin of the realm. A broader (read: whiter) audience had found a taste for hip-hop.

"It takes most people a lifetime career to establish what he established with one album."
– Busta Rhymes, in archival material on MTV.com

Biggie and Faith Evans, his wife from August 1994.
© ERIC JOHNSON / CORBIS

If 2Pac's grace was his ability to generate a homily or rebuke over any social ill that swam through his ken, Big's was his commitment to the material world. The last glimpses we have as an audience are of Biggie in the *Life After Death* days. Close to four hundred pounds by then, he became bigger than big in scope and waistline. A car accident in September 1996 left him wheelchair-ridden, then dependent on a cane. A rumored affair between Biggie's wife, Faith Evans, and Tupac galvanized the animosity between Shakur and Wallace, and the sudden death of Tupac shook Biggie to his core. This is Michael Corleone at the end of *The Godfather II* and before *III*, a man immobilized by actions and fate.

The Notorious B.I.G. greets the darkness with braggadocio and gallows humor. The music video for "Hypnotize," the lead single from *Life After Death*, has Biggie and Puff on the run from hitmen. A coy government-conspiracy vibe permeates the five-minute video. The unidentified assailants use radar and deploy black helicopters to track Big, Puffy, and their female companions in the first verse. In the second verse a horde of operatives on motorcycles and in military Humvees chase the pair as they drive a cherry-red BMW convertible backwards through city streets. During the video's conclusion, in the hidden underwater lair of Bad Boy Records, Biggie barely pivots on his cane as Puff leads the dancers in a jerky hora around the kingpin. The video documents a luxurious paranoia, one in which The Notorious B.I.G. barely evades the forces that would have him killed.

To choose between Tupac Shakur and The Notorious B.I.G. on a post-sonic, aesthetic level resembles, in a way, how one chooses to accept death. The seemingly omnipresent sunglasses Biggie wore in his last months, to me, reflect some general refusal of life's short lease. He's literally blocked out parts the world and refuses to show us his full range of expression. We can't see what he's focused on.

It could also come down to poses. 2Pac bared his body to the camera in a way Biggie never did. 2Pac offered himself in various states of emotion on his album covers: seated, flashing the "West Side" hand gesture; chin-stroking in contemplation; standing upright with every muscle coiled. 2Pac seemed so playful, so perpetually energetic in life because, at least according to his songs, the spiritual side of his existence mattered more. Biggie resembles the seventeenth-century paintings of Dutch merchants: men obsessed with the physical world and its tangible rewards because the spiritual world was filled with a great, predetermined void.

(Following pages) **Still Ain't Mad,** by Hugo Diaz. Digital painting, 2011. COURTESY OF THE ARTIST

Big Poppa, spray paint and acrylic. *POINT BLANK ART & DESIGN, LLC. WWW. POINTBLANKDESIGN.NET*

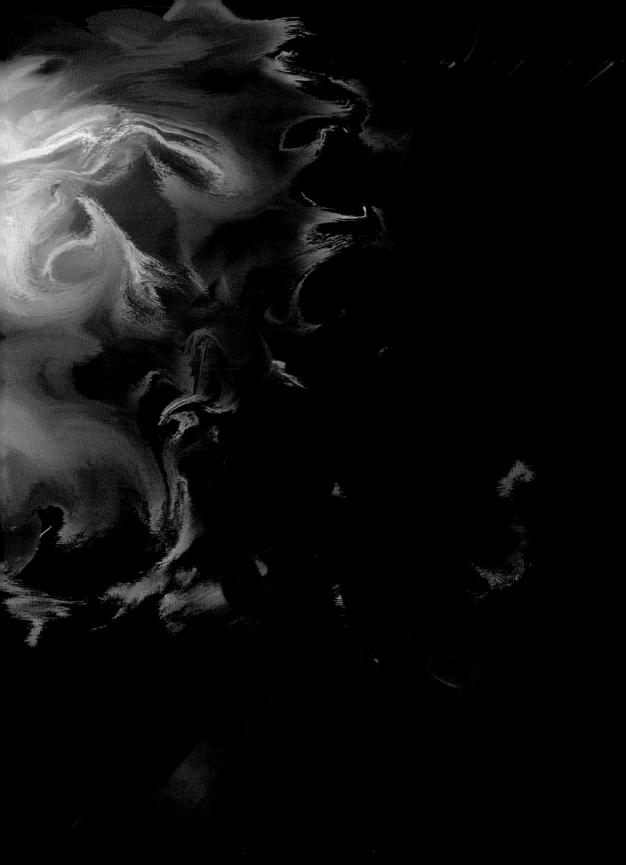

Chapter 4

RISE TO
POWER

2PAC

There was no Gatsby self-betterment through bootlegging. 2Pac was the rootless Western vagabond, heavily armed and alienated, loyal to a fault and quick to squeeze the trigger— manifest destiny in a Mercedes Benz. Dismiss any notions of him as the white-hatted hero. 2Pac's optimal colors were black and red, skin and blood. Like Clint Eastwood once croaked: every gun makes its own tune.

Biggie wrote fiction. Tupac was fiction. His biography is bumper cars, one altercation after another until the final ascension. Even a smooth limo ride could be time for some action. See his 1993 trip to Fox Studios to tape an episode of *In Living Color*—when the driver asked him to stop smoking weed, he pulled out a pistol and had his entourage thrash the grunt senseless. That same year, he beat up the Hughes Brothers over a role in *Menace II Society* and then had the audacity to brag about it on *Yo! MTV Raps*. Watch the video on YouTube. It's wild.

The previous year, his hotheadedness helped turn a celebration for Marin City's fiftieth anniversary into a gunfight, with a six-year-old accidentally shot and killed. Shakur's half-brother was arrested in connection with the murder, but the charges were dropped due to lack of evidence.

The incident came after an altercation with Bay Area police, his violence there another vestige of Tupac's Black Panther upbringing. Obviously, there was the shooting of the two off-duty police officers in Atlanta. The sexual assault charge.

"So many battlefield scars while driving in plush cars / This life as a rap star is nothin without heart."
—"Ambitionz Az a Ridah"

"Shakur . . . becomes the film's most magnetic figure." —the *New York Times* on *Juice*, 1992.

The miscellaneous other easily avoidable conflicts. Tupac's problems were his strengths. The ten-thousand-watt personality and passion made him a magnetic entertainer, but he came without a dimmer mode; he was built to ball until he fell.

The intensity became electric chair when he played Bishop in 1992's *Juice*. Biggie famously told *Vibe* that the last time he spoke to Tupac, he saw only Bishop. The path of Tupac's breakout character and his own arc neatly paralleled. Both became entranced by power, or juice, the intoxicating idea of getting away with whatever the fuck they wanted. The plot lines in Ernest Dickerson's script might well have been ripped from Tupac's journals. Harlem boy gets harassed by the police and

"Who shot me, but you punks didn't finish / Now you're 'bout to feel the wrath of a menace." – "Hit Em Up"

rival thugs and inevitably snaps. He decides that he won't take any more shit, gets a Glock, and starts wilding out.

Of course, Tupac never shot a bodega store owner dead or attempted to pick off his friends one by one. But you can see the fearlessness and rage in his eyes as Bishop and link the expression to his last years. Following his prison stint, he looked at Biggie as if Big were *Juice* character Q, the one-time ally who attempted to engineer his destruction. But Tupac had survived the Quad City attacks and wanted to wreak the revenge that Bishop never could.

Rappers had acted since 1983's *Wild Style*, a film that included Fab Five Freddy, Cold Crush Brothers, and Grandmaster Flash. The Fat Boys had their own string of movies. So did Kid 'n Play. Will Smith's performance on *The Fresh Prince of Bel-Air* was probably equally important to the mainstreaming of hip-hop as Vanilla Ice or MC Hammer's hits. And you have to pimp clap for

Ice Cube's performance as Doughboy in *Boyz n the Hood*. But Tupac was the first rapper who people actually took seriously as an actor.

"He's what they call a natural," John Singleton, the director of *Boyz n the Hood* and *Poetic Justice*, told *Vibe* in 1994. "You know, he's a real actor. He has all these methods and everything, philosophies about how a role should be played."

Long before he ever picked up the microphone, there was the role in *A Raisin in the Sun*. Later, there was the teenager at the elite Baltimore art school acting alongside Jada Pinkett. It was Pinkett's future husband, Will Smith, who may have been Shakur's perfect foil. Both parlayed Grammy-nominated rap careers into acting roles. But while Smith softened his hood side with self-deprecating humor, a constant smile, and anodyne lyrics, Shakur's goal was simultaneously to terrify and intrigue White America.

You can trace this same accommodationist vs. militant streak back to Booker T. Washington and W. E. B. Du Bois. I'd rather say that Will Smith lived up to the 2005 *Onion* headline, "Will Smith: The Black Man Everyone at Work Can Agree Upon," whereas Tupac was the man that America loved to hate. Ice Cube may have had a monopoly on that phrase, but it was no longer true. By 1995, Cube was the star of *Friday* and was well on his way to starring in Coors commercials with penguins. But Tupac was despised by hundreds of thousands of people until the day that he died.

Tupac's upbringing was practically as far removed from actual gangster life as spaghetti Western director Sergio Leone's was from the cowboy era.

Poetic Justice, with Janet Jackson, 1993.
© COLUMBIA / COURTESY EVERETT COLLECTION

As convincing as 2Pac's cold-blooded killer persona was, it could be caricatured. The *Don Killuminati* cover is actually a cartoon. He was method acting his life, freed from societal standards and taboo. His nerd days were incidental detail. And that only makes a more fascinating figure. Tupac was perennially reinventing himself. Not with the rational market-tested approach of Madonna, but through lunar mood swings, chaos, and free-fall.

"The actor in me [stemmed] from my fucked up childhood," Tupac said in the same 1994 *Vibe* profile. "The reason why I could get into acting was because it takes nothin' to get out of who I am to get into somebody else."

The film career offered Tupac access to a different stratosphere of celebrity. Even though his track got derailed because of his jail sentence and bad rep, it's inevitable that he would have evolved into an actor with a tux always ready for award show duty. At the very least, he would've been infinitely better than Ludacris in *Crash*. This otherness from the hip-hop world afforded him more power. Slick Rick wasn't getting Rikers visits from Madonna.

Controversy is the cheapest publicity possible, and Shakur attracted attention at levels only known by Oscar Wilde. Examine the chart debuts of the first three 2Pac albums: *2Pacalypse Now* (#64), *Strictly 4 My N.I.G.G.A.Z.* (#24), *Thug Life: Volume 1* (#42). *Me Against the World* was released while he was incarcerated. It premiered at the top of the *Billboard* charts.

Of course, *Me Against the World* spawned his biggest single (and arguably best song) to date in the top-10 "Dear Mama." But great songs can buy you positive reviews and occasionally radio play. They cannot buy you front-page headlines. The combination of 2Pac's Quad City shooting, his famous refusal to stay in the hospital, and his subsequent court appearance in a wheelchair molded his indestructible myth. The pictures were everywhere—the possessed grimace, the Rolex on his right wrist, gauze on his left, his head and leg bandaged, the wounds scarcely concealed by a Yankees beanie.

Tupac's end was imminent, but in 1995, that was opaque. He was Bo Jackson conquering baseball and football, but Bo didn't know Diddy. By twenty-three, Tupac had survived one shooting, shot two white police officers in the South and walked, been accused of making music that incited the murder of a Texas state trooper, and served time in upstate New York prisons. He had acted in major motion pictures and written songs that would later be enshrined in the Library of Congress. He was hero and villain, a walking, wounded Rorschach blot—someone the press and civil rights activist C. Delores Tucker (who was vocal in her opposition to Tupac's explicit lyrics and had fought the NAACP's nomination of Tupac for an Image Award) could revile, but the streets could worship. As he pointed out, "I loved the fact that I could go into any ghetto and be noticed and be known."

South Central L.A. rally, 1996—the apex of Tupac's rise.
PHOTO BY FRANK WIESE / ASSOCIATED PRESS

TUPAC'S LITERARY/MUSICAL/ CULTURAL INFLUENCES

EVAN MCGARVEY

1) NICCOLO MACHIAVELLI'S *THE PRINCE*

According to Eric Dyson's *Holler If You Hear Me*, Tupac read the renaissance Florentine writer's *The Prince* during his time in jail. Paranoid, wise, venial, brilliant, filled with recent history [the Borgia family's reign] and biblical reinterpretations [Moses as an emperor who took leadership by force], Machiavelli's book concerns itself with the education of would-be leaders and structures of empire. The book arrived for Tupac at the perfect time. He read it during a period of intense, self-directed education while behind bars. And on his release he joined a fraught, ultimately unsustainable empire: Death Row Records. Shakur even began to use the stage name Makaveli after his prison release. He intended for his album The Don Killuminati: *The 7 Day Theory* to introduce this new nom de plume to the world.

2) SHAKESPEAREAN TRAGEDY

In an interview with Chuck Philips in 1995, less than a week after his release from prison, Tupac mentioned that he read Shakespeare while incarcerated. In the interview, Shakur linked the cycle of violence and remorse in *Macbeth* to the songs of legendary Houston rapper Scarface. He compared *Romeo and Juliet*'s star-crossed lovers to the feud between the Crips and Bloods. In retrospect, the DNA of historic tragedy fills much of Tupac's work: friendships, betrayals, characters unable to see their own flaws, mass-scale violence. On a personal level, it's hard not to see Tupac's irreconcilable dichotomy of self—citizen and thug, lover and fighter—as a, well, tragic flaw.

3) THE AUTOBIOGRAPHY OF MALCOLM X FOR TUPAC'S INTERVIEWS

No pop artist outside of Bob Marley and the Beatles wielded the medium of the celebrity interview with the same purpose as Tupac. In interviews in the mid-1990s with journalists like Kevin Powell of *Vibe* and Chuck Philips of the *L.A. Times* (to name just two), Shakur held court. Few topics were beyond his rhetorical reach: his own education in the performing arts, expectations of black masculinity, the sexual and financial politics of hip-hop, his peers, his future, the American prison system, and "God's will." He could slough off previous claims like a chrysalis and present himself as a new man at the end of each article. Yet he was meticulous to leave a trail of development—telling Powell that while the Thug Life movement was foolish, "My intentions was always in the right place."

"We talk a lot about Malcolm X and Martin Luther King Jr., but it's time to be like them, as strong as them. They were mortal men like us and every one of us can be like them."—Tupac.

PHOTOGRAPH BY MARION S. TRIKOSKO / LIBRARY OF CONGRESS

Reading the interviews, I'm struck by how much they resemble the incandescent movements of tone and subject in *The Autobiography of Malcolm X*. The 1965 collaboration between Malcolm X and Alex Haley (the future author of *Roots*) uses the form of the autobiography in a way that brilliantly reflects the power of the subject matter. The evolution in Malcolm's names—Malcolm Little to Detroit Red to El-Hajj Malik El-Shabazz—resonates with Tupac's shifting pseudonyms. The sometimes adversarial, sometimes confessional relationship between Tupac and the press doesn't mirror at all Malcolm X's working relationship with Alex Haley, but I read both *The Autobiography* and Tupac's interview style as asymmetrically collaborative. Haley acts as a kind of invisible rudder for Malcolm, subsuming his own voice to Malcolm's and guiding the manuscript structurally. Tupac's interviewers were forced into a similar role, if only to help sculpt the waves of pull quotes and epiphanies that Shakur issued. Both the interviews and *The Autobiography* deliver what they promise: a powerful voice telling the story of a complicated life.

The love was mutual enough that Tupac attempted to launch an ill-fated urban reform program, T.H.U.G. L.I.F.E, complete with a twenty-six-bullet-point code of conduct. It included would-be aphorisms: every new jack to the game must know, a) he's going to get rich, b) he's going to jail, c) he's going to die. One crew's rat is every crew's rat. Rats are like a disease—sooner or

> "It's not like I idolize this one guy Machiavelli. I idolize that type of thinking where you do whatever's gonna make you achieve your goal."
>
> — *Vibe* magazine, September 1996

later we all get it, and they should too. The boys in blue don't run nothing; we do. Control the hood, make it safe for squares. No slanging to children or pregnant women. And "be a real ruff neck."

Never really enforced, the plan's pinnacle came at the Truce Picnic in California in 1992, where the leaders of the Bloods and Crips pledged allegiance to the code. By 1996, Tupac was recording for Death Row, protected by a snarling phalanx of Bloods and former cops who were arguably more gangster than the gangsters. Plus, he had aligned himself with the biggest gangster of all, Suge Knight, a Blood who applied mafia ethics to the music business.

In hindsight, the arrangement between Shakur and Knight could only have been temporary. Tupac was far too stubborn to submit to a higher terrestrial power for very long. Biggie was malleable enough to let Puffy help tame the street corner spitter into a polished dance-floor-friendly singles machine. While Shock G of Digital Underground and later Jimmy Iovine and Suge Knight

helped steer 2Pac toward mass appeal, he ultimately met the mainstream on his own terms. True pop concessions were unthinkable. He died at the solstice of his fame, so there were no embarrassing attempts to stay current or soften his style. That was what Ja Rule was for.

During his turbulent final two years, Machiavelli's *The Prince* prominently underwrote Tupac's philosophy. His idealism had eroded into a barbaric realism. He saw himself as the enlightened tyrant rising to the top out of virtue, commanding respect and forcing others to bow down to his will (and Death Row). He nodded his head and strove to go directly to what Machiavelli called the "effectual truth of the thing, [rather] than to the imagination of it." It was the perfect melding of his raps with a ruling strategy. Machiavelli morphed into Makaveli, but both the writer and the warrior shared a few things: the need to plot and scheme, self-sufficiency, and the importance of showing neither mercy nor weakness.

Cova da Moura district of Lisbon, Portugal, 2007. *© NACHO DOCE / REUTERS / CORBIS*

BIGGIE

When we talk about the lives of Christopher Wallace and Tupac Shakur and we compare the rises of The Notorious B.I.G and 2Pac, we talk about the subject of ascendance. That is, we talk about how adolescence becomes adulthood and how rhyming for friends becomes rapping for millions. We talk about the initial goals of the artist and the realities and ramifications of trying to make those goals real.

Making an argument for Biggie and 2Pac's interwoven personal and artistic narratives becomes extremely difficult here. Not just because 2Pac had released two solo albums and a group album, *Thug Life: Volume 1*, before Biggie's debut in 1994. And not just because their first years as artists and men were as dissimilar as their final years were closely intertwined. It is the dissonance between the subject of ascendance in each artist's music and the path each man took to the peak of hip-hop celebrity that makes choice here so difficult. What Tupac and Biggie said on record doesn't match up with the realities of their respective rises from young artists to pop culture celebrities.

For The Notorious B.I.G., the musical mythology unfolds like so: the innocent, impoverished young man dares to become the hustler who labors his way to mid-level dealer, who cleaves and claws his way to a Mafioso throne.

Christopher Wallace the man benefited from more than one serendipitous break, whether it was access to the improvised basement and living room recording studios in Brooklyn he'd hang out in after he'd finish hustling; meeting DJ 50 Grand, who both coaxed Biggie into recording a tape and hectored the legendary DJ Mister Cee to listen to the tape; or benefiting from the young Sean Combs' foresight to build a label around Biggie when Combs was fired from Uptown Records in 1993. The two moves

Street Phenomenon Biggie, by Daniel York AKA TheDigArtisT. Digital media, 2011.
COURTESY OF THE ARTIST. www.redbubble.com/people/thedigartist/shop

"Keep on pushing the boundaries and reaching for higher heights." — Sean Combs, with Biggie in 1995. © BUREAU L.A. COLLECTION / SYGMA / CORBIS

Wallace made in his life—onto the street and into the studio—gave him the bulk of his material: how a schoolboy hustles and how a hustler raps. In life, Wallace moved swiftly from hustler to rising star to smash debutant to icon. In many ways, the lyrical avatar of Biggie faces a harder road to underworld success than Christopher Wallace did in the rap game. The man was far luckier than the character he created.

In contrast, 2Pac was the artist who thrived in many spheres. He changed from childhood stage actor at the Baltimore School for the Arts to Digital Underground backup dancer to underground MC. An artistic and moral vision catalyzed the start of his career as an MC. His first single was 1991's "Brenda's Got A Baby," a cautionary tale and plea. The menace and first-person violence that shaped Biggie's music from the outset infused the second-half of Shakur's output with new energy. His post-prison double album, 1996's *All Eyez On Me*, billows with a weary vanity, a mood largely foreign to the 2Pac of 1991's *2pocalypse Now* and 1993's *Strictly 4 My N.I.G.G.A.Z.*

This book has previously covered some details of Christopher Wallace's early life. Since we're now going to deal with more of Biggie's real-life incidents and their rendering in verse, I want to direct readers to an invaluable book, a book I've cited previously here and have consulted regularly in my own reading: Cheo Hodari Coker's *Unbelievable: The Life, Death, and Afterlife of The Notorious B.I.G.*

Coker's interviews with (among others) Voletta Wallace, Faith Evans, DJ Mister Cee, Lil' Cease, Touré, and a dozen others are vital, revealing reads and were key in linking the chronology of Biggie's life with his music. Coker's summary of key passages in Wallace's life and his encyclopedic list of recordings are similarly useful. For a second-order effort like the one I'm making, an effort made up of song analysis and thematic arguments, strong

Madison Square Garden, 1995. PHOTO BY DAVID CORIO / RED FERNS / GETTY IMAGES

BIGGIE'S LITERARY/MUSICAL/ CULTURAL INFLUENCES

EVAN
MCGARVEY

1) *THE GODFATHER'S* MICHAEL CORLEONE

The protagonist of Francis Ford Coppola's *The Godfather* overlaps with Biggie's life and art. As men, the doted-upon Christopher Wallace and favored son Michael, played by Al Pacino, were afforded good educations and slotted into trajectories that promised to pull them up the American ladder. In art, their evolutions took two parts: in the first, from apprentice to savant; in the second, from boss to titan. *Ready To Die* and *The Godfather* begin with Biggie and Michael initiating themselves into crime and end in sacrifices: Biggie's attempted suicide, Michael's betrayal of Diane Keaton's Kay. Like a sequel, *Life After Death* begins with a voice intoning, "Previously on *Ready To Die*. . . ." And like *The Godfather II*, *Life After Death* leaps from the coming-of-age tale into the epic. Both the film and the album juxtapose childhood scenes with adult transactions and linger on fading hopes for transcendence (the Corleone family going legal; Biggie escaping the crack game). The endings? Bleaker than bleak. Michael has his own brother killed; Biggie envisages his own death.

Big Daddy Kane, 1988. Big is just one of countless rappers he's influenced.
PHOTO BY DAVID CORIO / REDFERNS / GETTY IMAGES

2) BIG DADDY KANE

Biggie built his yachts, millions, and mansions from Brooklyn's original player blueprint. Kane was already four albums deep before Biggie put songs on wax for the first time in 1993. Kane's flow shifted gears smoother than an Aston Martin—he moved from one-two boom-bap to more languid, catchphrase-driven lines without a

Goodfellas. © MOVIESTORE COLLECTION LTD / ALAMY

pause for breath. Biggie emulated Kane's verbal versatility in
his earlier songs. On "Party and Bullshit" the first verse taps
out a methodical, almost kick-snare pattern of words while the
second and third lean on less stressed phrases. That movement
is pure Kane. Biggie wasn't the only admirer in his crew. Puffy
borrowed from the arrangement of Kane's albums: soul and R&B
from the recent past glossed up and chopped up for a one-man
cipher. It must have been fate that allowed DJ Mister Cee, Kane's
longtime man behind the turntable, to discover the young B.I.G.

3) MARTIN SCORSESE'S *CASINO* AND *GOODFELLAS*

More contemporary than the *Godfather* films, and more glamorous,
Martin Scorsese's 1990s gangster films *Casino* and *Goodfellas*
get direct references from the Bad Boy family. In the untimely
career closing "You're Nobody ('Till Somebody Kills You),"
Biggie croons, "Watch *Casino*, I'm the hip-hop version of Nicky."
Nick Santoro, Joe Pesci's unhinged capo, pouts and prances in
ways Biggie's killers don't. But like Pesci in both *Casino* and
Goodfellas, Biggie often instigated a song's chain of violence,
unprepared for blowback. The aesthetics between Scorsese's
gangsters and Biggie's fit perfectly. The dripping, wide-screen
opulence of songs like "I Love The Dough," "Goin' Back To Cali,"
and "Big Poppa" beg for Scorsese's steady cam. Puffy makes the
admiration transparent on 1997's "It's All About The Benjamins"
when he chirps *"Goodfellas!"* at the start of the song.

primary reporting is essential. Coker's book now seems like the definitive textual record of Christopher Wallace's life, and readers who want to learn the full story behind the incidents and anecdotes mentioned here would be best served by a copy of *Unbelievable*.

One of the great mysteries of F. Scott Fitzgerald's *The Great Gatsby* is the book's refusal to show the poverty of Jay Gatz the Dakota farm boy. We're shown the shirts and parties and champagne in West Egg, but nothing of how the bootlegging title character went from Gatz to Gatsby. The character's past struggles float under the glittering surface of his finished life.

Consider that gap, that mystery, against the horrifying explicitness of Biggie Smalls: "I got the Calico with the black talons / loaded in the clip / so I can rip through the ligaments / put the fuckers in a bad predicament." And, a few lines later, "blood stains on what remains of his jacket." These lines, from "Warning" on *Ready To Die*, give us total access to the horrors of mid-level dealers. Biggie's status affords him just enough connections to hear from "Pop at the barbershop" that men plan to rob him, "stick him like flypaper." But his same status—in the game, not yet made—means he himself has to get his hands bloody. He's Michael Corleone reaching behind the toilet tank for the gun with the taped-up grip.

The word *predicament* in those lines reflects the trend of sinister understatement in Biggie's scenes of violence. While blessed with an eye that casts a lyric scene into an immediate space—Biggie reminds me of the poet Robert Lowell's ability to summon a specific setting (in Lowell's case, a fading WASP milieu) through diction and detail—an element of dramatis personae anchors the violence on *Ready To Die*. That is, Biggie understands dramatis personae the way poets understands it: the *I* of a song is not a simple stand-in for the author. The *I* can be a wholly invented character or an avatar that overlaps with the author in places. If you think the *I* in every Biggie song is all Christopher Wallace, all the time, you would be, to steal a phrase from the artist himself, dead wrong.

Biggie's voice on the album attempts to sound nonchalant about the horror, but he doesn't totally convince. His eye stays with scenes for just a beat too long—that bloody jacket—and his voice doubles back on itself. Biggie's voice has to psyche itself up for murder; it has to convince itself it's doing what's necessary. When he uses the first-person plural on "Things Done Changed"—"We get hype and shit, start lighting shit"—it's as if he's trying to convince himself that everyone around is just like him.

In real life, however, doubt doesn't figure much into Christopher Wallace's rapid ascent to stardom. A spate of arrests around 1990—a gun possession arrest in Brooklyn in 1989, a cocaine possession charge in North Carolina in 1991, which led to a jail stint—galvanized him. Those events became grist for the mill.

The Bad Boy crew: Craig Mack, Sean Combs, Biggie. 1994. © CHI MODU, DIVERSE IMAGES / CORBIS

Biggie claimed in a 1994 interview with Touré in the *New York Times* that drug charges put him in jail for nine months (a figure repeated by the *Associated Press* in 1996 and by the *Times* in a 1997 article on his murder). Cathy Scott, in *The Murder of Biggie Smalls*, reports that his mother wired him a $25,000 bail bond and his jail stint was only a few days. Although the legal system stymied Christopher Wallace the man, it couldn't hold back the artist. The rap world immediately recognized the rising star.

Biggie in the 1997 hip-hop documentary *Rhyme & Reason*. He was interviewed for the movie, which was released just four days before he was killed. *PHOTOFEST*

In his interview with Coker for *Unbelievable*, DJ Mister Cee claimed that when DJ 50 Grand, part of the Old Gold Crew with whom Big rapped in between corner sessions, brought him a demo of a young man flowing over a sample of The Emotions' "Blind Alley" (a sample also used in Big Daddy Kane's legendary "Ain't No Half Steppin'") in the fall of 1991, he heard "a message from God." The young man on the tape was Biggie Smalls.

Mister Cee knew talent. And he knew people would recognize and admire the simultaneously nimble and booming baritone. After recording a proper demo with Big, he contacted *The Source*, whose editors did not hesitate to put Biggie in their "Unsigned Hype" column, a column with an absurd rate of return that had previously featured Mobb Deep, DMX, and Common Sense (now known as Common). From there, Sean Combs, then a rising A&R man at Uptown Records, heard the demo. A partnership was born.

Unlike contemporary MCs who habitually aired grievances about the "rap game" and its promises, betrayals, and allure, Biggie did not devote many lines to the business of recording music. He marks his own transition from hustling to rapping, but the lyrical craft goes without comment. When his lyrical ability is discussed on his records, other voices do the praising. On "Sky's The Limit," he constructs a persona to, essentially, introduce himself, "I'd like to welcome to the stage / the lyrically acclaimed. . . ."

That song, from the colossal posthumous double-album *Life After Death*, provides a chart of Biggie's evolution. The first verse covers childhood; the second, Big's breaking into the drug game; the third, the formation of his own crew. It's convenient to read the song as an elegy to his hustling days. But because any biographic reading of Christopher Wallace's life shows that Wallace himself never progressed beyond the rank of mid-level dealer, and because we know exaggeration helped him unfurl the events of his life into art, the song takes on a different subtext.

I think we can hear the song as an extended metaphor for Biggie's ascension as an MC *and* as a hustler. The song opens with a moment of imitation: "I'm sewing tigers on my shirt." Imitation stands at the center of the emerging artist's world. Emulating Big Daddy Kane and Rakim's flow, their ability to break apart sentences and phrases across lines, emphasizing different syllables, gave Biggie a model for how to rap.

Later in the verse he teaches himself how to balance wisdom and revenge: "Play your position, here come my intuition / Go in this nigga pocket, rob him while his friend watching." A nod to stealing lines and techniques, but stealing them carefully? I think so. Biggie brought subtlety and predatory timing to battle raps—he diffused 2Pac's furious taunts about knocking up Faith Evans with a coy lyrical shrug: "If Faith have twins she probably have two Pac's" (his guest verse on "Brooklyn's Finest" from Jay-Z's 1996 debut *Reasonable Doubt*). He regurgitated a taunt from Raekwon by using the same instrument of torture—bleach—on "Kick In The Door."

In the second verse, seemingly every line deals with transformation. He makes his choice to go from crack to rap explicit: "Ain't no telling where this felon is headed." Old crews get left behind. Without disrespecting the figures in his rear view—Old Gold Crew, etc.—he leaves an imaginary, petty drug ring: "I was a shame, my crew was lame / I had enough heart for most of them." Women get left behind too. When he debuted he rapped about love and sex and loyalty. *Ready To Die*'s "Me & My Bitch" ended with a Morrissey-esque plea to "fuckin' die together." At the apex of the rap game, those feelings had changed. Clearly. On "Sky's The Limit" he says, "Plus, I'm fuckin' bitches ain't my homegirls now." Fitting, since the sex-centric jam from *Life After Death* is "Nasty Boy," steely and sweaty and completely unengaged.

The physical details of "Sky's The Limit" are harder to translate. There's no analogy for the song's catalogue of drug use: "some use pipes, others use injections." Still, there's an intermingling between Christopher Wallace's two worlds on the song. He looks backs at the world filled with corners and users while on top of the safer, artistic one. The song's then-and-now contrasts don't just deal with age and development; they imply how the crack trade has informed Biggie's life in the rap game.

As The Notorious B.I.G. reached the heights of hip-hop fame, he kept his previous lives internalized as a cache of metaphors and images. Laid bare, the divides between his youth and his prematurely weathered adulthood resonate in his music. In contrast, 2Pac treated each stage of his professional career as a rebirth. He didn't climb so much as he leapt. The trail of Biggie's craft and reception feels more intimate because his ascent felt so rapid. Another truth from Fitzgerald: American lives don't have second acts. As much as Biggie saw himself as having many, perhaps it really was all a dream. Maybe his life and his music embody one move, the shooting star who thrills in act one and whose path stops at its apex, destroyed by fate.

Billboard® HOT R&B SINGLES™

MAY 10, 1997

COMPILED FROM A NATIONAL SAMPLE OF R&B RADIO AIRPLAY MONITORED BY BROADCAST DATA SYSTEMS, R&B RADIO PLAYLISTS, AND RETAIL SINGLE SALES COLLECTED, COMPILED, AND PROVIDED BY SoundScan®

THIS WEEK	LAST WEEK	2 WKS AGO	WKS. ON CHART	TITLE / PRODUCER (SONGWRITER)	ARTIST / LABEL & NUMBER/PROMOTION LABEL	PEAK POSITION
1	1	1	3	★★★ No. 1 ★★★ HYPNOTIZE (3 weeks at No. 1) / D.ANGELETTIE,R.LAWRENCE,S.COMBS (C.WALLACE,S.COMBS,D.ANGELETTIE,R.LAWRENCE,A.ARMER,R.BADAZZ,R.WALTERS,D.DAVIS)	◆ THE NOTORIOUS B.I.G. / (C) (D) BAD BOY 79092/ARISTA	1
2	19	—	2	G.H.E.T.T.O.U.T. / R.KELLY (R.KELLY)	◆ CHANGING FACES / (C) (D) (T) BIG BEAT 98026/ATLANTIC	2
3	3	8	10	I BELONG TO YOU (EVERY TIME I SEE YOUR FACE) / G.BAILLERGEAU,V.MERRITT (GERALD BAILLERGEAU)	◆ ROME / (C) (D) (V) RCA 64759	3
4	2	4	11	CUPID / A.HENNINGS (A.HENNINGS,C.SILLS,D.JONES,M.KEITH,M.SCANDRICK,Q.PARKER)	◆ 112 / (C) (D) (V) BAD BOY 79087/ARISTA	2
5	5	3	4	MY BABY DADDY / B.AGEE (L.AGEE,B.AGEE,M.WHITE,A.MCKAY)	◆ B-ROCK & THE BIZZ / (C) (D) (T) (X) TONY MERCEDES/LAFACE 24221/ARISTA	3
6	8	13	17	RETURN OF THE MACK ● / M.MORRISON,P.CHILL (M.MORRISON,P.CHILL)	◆ MARK MORRISON / (C) (D) (T) (X) ATLANTIC 84868	6
7	6	5	11	BIG DADDY ● / T.DOFAT,HEAVY D (T.DOFAT,HEAVY D,H.BROWN)	◆ HEAVY D / (C) (D) (T) UPTOWN 56039/UNIVERSAL	5
8	4	2	10	FOR YOU I WILL (FROM "SPACE JAM") ● / D.FOSTER (D.WARREN)	◆ MONICA / (C) (D) ROWDY/WARNER SUNSET 87003/ATLANTIC	2
9	9	6	19	IN MY BED ▲ / D.SIMMONS (R.BROWN,R.B.STACY,D.SIMMONS)	◆ DRU HILL / (C) (D) ISLAND 854854	1
10	13	14	7	FOR YOU / B.J.EASTMOND (K.LERUM)	◆ KENNY LATTIMORE / (C) (D) COLUMBIA 78456	10
11	16	—	2	DON'T WANNA BE A PLAYER (FROM "BOOTY CALL") / R.JERKINS (J.THOMAS,J.SKINNER,R.JERKINS,J.TEJEDA,M.WILLIAMS)	◆ JOE / (C) (D) JIVE 42450	11
12	7	9	13	GET IT TOGETHER ● / D.JONES (D.JONES)	◆ 702 / (C) (D) (V) BIV 10 860612/MOTOWN	3
13	11	11	15	WHAT'S ON TONIGHT / DEVANTE (M.JORDAN,DEVANTE,J.E.JONES)	◆ MONTELL JORDAN / (C) (D) (T) DEF JAM 574032/MERCURY	7
14	NEW ▶		1	★★★ HOT SHOT DEBUT ★★★ THINKING OF YOU/LET'S GET DOWN / TONY TONI TONE,QUICK,G-ONE (R.SAADIQ,D.WIGGINS,T.C.RILEY,D.BLAKE,G.ARCHIE JR.)	◆ TONY TONI TONE / (C) (D) (T) (V) MERCURY 574382	14
15	12	7	16	CAN'T NOBODY HOLD ME DOWN ▲2 / C.BROADY,N.MYRICK,S.COMBS,STEVIE J. (S.COMBS,S.JORDAN,C.BROADY,N.MYRICK,M.BETHA,G.PRESTOPINO,M.WILDER,S.ROBINSON)	◆ PUFF DADDY (FEATURING MASE) / (C) (D) (T) (X) BAD BOY 79083/ARISTA	1
16	15	15	7	I LOVE ME SOME HIM/I DON'T WANT TO / SOULSHOCK,KARLIN,R.KELLY (A.MARTIN,G.STEWART,SOULSHOCK,KARLIN,R.KELLY)	◆ TONI BRAXTON / (C) (D) LAFACE 24229/ARISTA	12
17	10	10	13	I'LL BE ● / POKE & TONE (S.CARTER,J.C.OLIVIER,S.J.BARNES,A.WINBUSH,R.MOORE)	◆ FOXY BROWN FEATURING JAY-Z / (C) (D) (T) VIOLATOR/DEF JAM 574028/MERCURY	5
18	14	12	7	YOU DON'T HAVE TO HURT NO MORE / MINT CONDITION (K.LEWIS)	◆ MINT CONDITION / (C) (D) (T) (V) (X) PERSPECTIVE 587564/A&M	10
19	NEW ▶		1	BLOOD ON THE DANCE FLOOR / M.JACKSON,T.RILEY (M.JACKSON,T.RILEY)	◆ MICHAEL JACKSON / (C) (D) (T) (V) (X) EPIC 78007	19
20	18	16	16	ON & ON ● / B.POWER,J.JAMAL (E.BADU,J.JAMAL)	◆ ERYKAH BADU / (C) (D) (T) KEDAR 56002/UNIVERSAL	1
21	21	19	15	EVERY TIME I CLOSE MY EYES ● / BABYFACE (BABYFACE)	◆ BABYFACE / (C) (D) (V) (X) EPIC 78485	5
22	22	20	12	HARD TO SAY I'M SORRY ● / BABYFACE (R.CETERA,D.FOSTER)	◆ AZ YET FEATURING PETER CETERA / (C) (D) (T) (V) (X) LAFACE 24223/ARISTA	20
23	32	36	5	★★★ GREATEST GAINER/SALES ★★★ COME ON / D.ALLAMBY (B.LAWRENCE,D.ALLAMBY)	◆ BILLY LAWRENCE FEATURING MC LYTE / (C) (D) (T) (X) EASTWEST 64239/EEG	23
24	20	18	9	I SHOT THE SHERIFF ● / WARREN G (B.MARLEY,L.PARKER,TONI C.,E.SERMON,P.SMITH)	◆ WARREN G / (C) (D) (T) G FUNK/DEF JAM 573564/MERCURY	16
25	17	17	10	LET IT GO (FROM "SET IT OFF") / K.CROUCH (K.CROUCH,G.MCKINNEY,R.PENNON)	◆ RAY J / (C) (D) (M) (T) (X) EASTWEST 64206/EEG	17
26	27	26	13	THE THEME (IT'S PARTY TIME) / D.ANGELETTIE,R.LAWRENCE (T.LEE,D.ANGELETTIE,R.LAWRENCE,C.HARMON,C.NAPPOLEON,J.LLOYD)	◆ TRACEY LEE / (C) (D) (T) BYSTORM 56114/UNIVERSAL	19
27	31	28	28	DA' DIP ● / FREAK NASTY (FREAK NASTY)	◆ FREAK NASTY / (C) (T) (X) HARD HOOD/POWER 0112/TRIAD	16
28	23	23	35	LET ME CLEAR MY THROAT / DJ KOOL,S.JANIS,F.DERBY (DJ KOOL)	◆ DJ KOOL / (C) (T) (X) CLR/AMERICAN 17441/WARNER BROS.	21
29	34	35	12	FULL OF SMOKE / CHRISTION (POETRY MAN)	◆ CHRISTION / (C) (D) (T) (X) ROC-A-FELLA/DEF JAM 573786/MERCURY	29
30	24	21	9	HEAD OVER HEELS / M.CAREY,POKE & TONE (M.CAREY,N.JONES,S.BARNES,J.C.OLIVIER,M.WILLIAMS,S.MOLTKE)	◆ ALLURE FEATURING NAS / (C) (D) (T) TRACK MASTERS/CRAVE 78522/EPIC	17
31	44	55	6	★★★ GREATEST GAINER/AIRPLAY ★★★ CALL ME (FROM "BOOTY CALL") / SHORTY B,TOO SHORT (T.SHAW,K.JONES,S.JORDAN)	◆ TOO SHORT & LIL' KIM / (T) JIVE 42447*	31
32	37	37	8	STEP INTO A WORLD (RAPTURE'S DELIGHT) / J.WEST (L.PARKER,J.WEST,D.HARRY,C.STEIN,H.PALMER)	◆ KRS-ONE / (T) JIVE 42442*	32
33	26	22	9	REQUEST LINE / KAY GEE,D.LIGHTY (R.NEUFVILLE,K.GEE,D.LIGHTY,N.ASHFORD,V.SIMPSON)	◆ ZHANE / (C) (D) (T) (X) ILLTOWN 860614/MOTOWN	9
34	25	25	5	JAZZY BELLE / ORGANIZED NOIZE (ORGANIZED NOIZE,A.BENJAMIN,A.PATTON)	◆ OUTKAST / (C) (D) (T) (X) LAFACE 24224/ARISTA	25
35	30	27	22	I BELIEVE I CAN FLY (FROM "SPACE JAM") ▲ / R.KELLY (R.KELLY)	◆ R. KELLY / (C) (D) (T) (V) (X) WARNER SUNSET/ATLANTIC 42422/JIVE	1
36	29	29	10	JUST THE WAY YOU LIKE IT / STEVIE J. (S.JORDAN,K.PRICE,STUART,GORRIE,WHITE,FERRONE)	◆ TASHA HOLIDAY / (C) (D) (T) MCA 55090	29
37	28	24	12	I'M NOT FEELING YOU / FUNKMASTER FLEX (M.BRYANT,J.SYLVESTER,F.HARVEY)	◆ YVETTE MICHELE / (C) (D) (T) LOUD 64790	12
38	39	—	2	SPIRIT / L.SEACER,B.STEELE (L.SEACER,B.STEELE,C.MACK)	◆ SOUNDS OF BLACKNESS FEATURING CRAIG MACK / (C) (D) PERSPECTIVE 587574/A&M	38
39	33	34	36	WHAT KIND OF MAN WOULD I BE ● / MINT CONDITION (L.WADDELL)	◆ MINT CONDITION / (C) (D) (V) (X) PERSPECTIVE 587558/A&M	2
40	36	31	10	GANGSTAS MAKE THE WORLD GO ROUND / ICE CUBE (ICE CUBE,MACK 10,W.C.,C.SAMSON,T.BELL,L.CREED)	◆ WESTSIDE CONNECTION / (C) (D) (T) LENCH MOB 53264/PRIORITY	30
41	35	41	3	STOP THE GUNFIGHT / TRAPP (T.SHAKUR,THE NOTORIOUS B.I.G.,J.PARKER)	TRAPP FEATURING 2PAC, NOTORIOUS B.I.G. / (C) DEFF TRAPP 9269/INTERSOUND	35
42	38	33	27	DON'T LET GO (LOVE) (FROM "SET IT OFF") ▲ / ORGANIZED NOIZE (ORGANIZED NOIZE,A.MARTIN,I.MATIAS,M.ETHERIDGE)	◆ EN VOGUE / (C) (D) (M) (T) (V) (X) EASTWEST 64231/EEG	1
43	45	45	6	DON'T KEEP WASTING MY TIME / T.PENDERGRASS,J.SALAMONE (J.SALAMONE,T.PENDERGRASS,J.YUDKIN)	TEDDY PENDERGRASS / (C) (D) SUREFIRE 18002	43
44	NEW ▶		1	FEMININITY / CHRISTIAN (E.BENET,C.WARREN)	◆ ERIC BENET / (C) (D) (V) WARNER BROS. 17571	44
45	NEW ▶		1	GET YOUR GROOVE ON (FROM "BAPS") / M.A.SAULSBERRY (P.WHITE,HUTCHINS,FLETCHER,SMITH)	◆ GYRL / (C) (D) (T) (X) SILAS 55334/MCA	45
46	47	—	2	FEELIN' IT / SKI (S.CARTER,D.WILLS)	◆ JAY-Z / (C) (D) (T) ROC-A-FELLA 53272/PRIORITY	46
47	53	53	5	GONNA LET U KNOW / TIZONE (TIZONE)	◆ LIL BUD & TIZONE FEATURING KEITH SWEAT / (C) (D) (T) ISLAND 854914	47
48	57	68	3	SOMETIMES / THE BRAND NEW HEAVIES (KINCAID,GARRETT)	◆ THE BRAND NEW HEAVIES / (C) (T) (X) DELICIOUS VINYL 4009/RED ANT	48
49	40	30	12	GHETTO LOVE ● / J.DUPRI (DA BRAT,L.PARKER,A.COLEANDRO,EL DEBARGE,C.RIDDENHOUR,H.SHOCKLEE)	◆ DA BRAT FEATURING T-BOZ / (C) (D) (T) (X) SO SO DEF 78527/COLUMBIA	11
50	55	—	2	IT MUST BE LOVE / B.WILSON (J.FOOTMAN,J.WIEDER)	◆ ROBIN S. / (C) (D) (T) BIG BEAT 95601/ATLANTIC	50
51	54	61	13	THAT'S RIGHT / T.MCLNTOSH (T.MCLNTOSH)	◆ DJ TAZ FEATURING RAHEEM THE DREAM / (C) (T) (X) BREAKAWAY/SUCCESS 58641/EMI	51
52	41	32	7	SHO NUFF / J.PHA (S.ARRINGTON,P.ALEXANDER,W.ROGERS)	◆ TELA FEATURING EIGHTBALL & MJG / (C) (D) (T) SUAVE HOUSE 1602/RELATIVITY	32
53	NEW ▶		1	IF U STAY READY / DJ QUIK,R.BACON,G-I (SUGA FREE,DJ QUIK,PLAYA HAM,R.BACON)	◆ SUGA FREE / (C) (D) (T) UNFADEABLE/SHEPPARD LANE 854976/ISLAND	53
54	42	40	13	SUMTHIN' SUMTHIN' (FROM "LOVE JONES") / MUSZE (MUSZE,WARE)	◆ MAXWELL / (T) COLUMBIA 78477*	23
55	52	50	20	I BELIEVE IN YOU AND ME/SOMEBODY BIGGER THAN YOU AND I (FROM "THE PREACHER'S WIFE") ▲ / M.WARREN,D.FOSTER,W.HOUSTON,R.MINOR (D.WOLFERT,S.LINZER,J.LANGE,H.HEATH,S.BURKE)	◆ WHITNEY HOUSTON / (C) (D) (M) (T) (V) (X) ARISTA 13293	4
56	51	51	14	I ALWAYS FEEL LIKE (SOMEBODY'S WATCHING ME) / MO B DICK,KLC,CRAIG B (MASTER P,SILKK THE SHOCKER,MIA X)	◆ TRU FEAT. ICE CREAM MAN (MASTER P) / (C) (D) (T) NO LIMIT 53261/PRIORITY	42
57	48	52	19	TEARS / A.WINBUSH,R.ISLEY (BABYFACE)	◆ THE ISLEY BROTHERS / (C) (D) T-NECK 854862/ISLAND	12
58	77	—	2	SO GOOD / B.HILL (MERRITT,E.YANCEY)	◆ ERICKA YANCEY / (C) (D) RCA 64816	58
59	59	59	3	LOVE IN AN ELEVATOR / TROY-TAYLOR,C.FARRAR (T.TAYLOR,C.FARRAR,C.THOMAS)	◆ JOHNNY GILL / (C) (D) MOTOWN 860626	59
60	43	38	9	STEP BY STEP (FROM "THE PREACHER'S WIFE") ● / S.LIPSON (A.LENNOX)	◆ WHITNEY HOUSTON / (C) (D) (M) (T) (V) (X) ARISTA 13312	29
61	66	71	13	EMOTIONS / THE LEGENDARY TRAXSTER (THE LEGENDARY TRAXSTER)	◆ TWISTA / (C) (D) (M) (T) (X) CREATOR'S WAY/BIG BEAT 98025/ATLANTIC	61
62	62	65	8	SEEIN' IS BELIEVING / DRED SCOTT (A.EVANS,DRED SCOTT)	◆ ADRIANA EVANS / (C) (D) (T) PMP 64780/LOUD	62
63	68	72	4	KEEP IT ON THE REAL / T.CAPONE (A.HENRY)	◆ 3X KRAZY / (C) (D) NOO TRYBE 38584/VIRGIN	63
64	65	—	2	G.O.D. PT. III / MOBB DEEP (JOHNSON,MUCHITA,COOPER,MORODER)	◆ MOBB DEEP / (C) (D) (T) LOUD 64833	64
65	64	56	6	SWEET LOVE / M.J.POWELL (A.BAKER,L.A.JOHNSON,G.BIAS)	◆ ELEMENTS OF LIFE / (C) (D) RCA 64753	56
66	60	60	12	T.O.N.Y. (TOP OF NEW YORK) / N.MYRICK,C.BROADY (K.HOLLEY,V.SANTIAGO,P.L.CHAPMAN)	◆ CAPONE-N-NOREAGA / (C) (D) (T) PENALTY 7193/TOMMY BOY	56
67	56	47	16	WHATEVA MAN / E.SERMON (E.SERMON,R.NOBLE)	◆ REDMAN / (C) (D) (T) DEF JAM 574026/MERCURY	18
68	74	74	7	IF TOMORROW NEVER COMES / L.PETTIS,H.LEE (K.BLAZY,G.BROOKS)	JOOSE / (C) (D) (X) FLAVOR UNIT/EASTWEST 64195/EEG	68
69	75	75	7	WU-RENEGADES / 4TH DISCIPLE (D.DEVALLE,J.GRANT,T.HAMLIN,S.MURRAY,S.BOUGARD)	◆ KILLARMY / (C) (D) (T) WU-TANG 53267/PRIORITY	69
70	61	63	10	NO ONE KNOWS ABOUT A GOOD THING (YOU DON'T HAVE TO CRY) / D.SIMMONS (D.SIMMONS,C.MAYFIELD)	CURTIS MAYFIELD / (C) (D) WARNER BROS. 17406	61
71	67	64	14	DO G'S GET TO GO TO HEAVEN? / M.MOSLEY (R.SERRELL,M.MOSLEY)	◆ RICHIE RICH / (C) (D) (T) OAKLAND HILLS 41510/DEF JAM 574030/MERCURY	37
72	NEW ▶		1	LIKE THIS AND LIKE THAT (FROM "THE 6TH MAN") / EMOSIA (EMOSIA,M.LORELLO)	◆ LAKIESHA BERRI / (C) HOLLYWOOD 164014	72
73	76	76	3	NO ONE BUT YOU / D.MANO,E.E.Q.QUINONES (V.VASQUEZ,D.MANO,S.AKIEN)	◆ VERONICA (FEATURING CRAIG MACK) / (T) H.O.L.A. 341014*/ISLAND	73
74	78	66	9	MAKE UP YOUR MIND / D.HALL (N.JOHNSON,C.LIGGIO,R.AYERS,S.STRIPLIN,B.BEDFORD)	◆ ASSORTED PHLAVORS FEATURING BIG DADDY KANE / (C) (D) (T) HALL OF FAME 78410/EPIC	58
75	97	89	4	U CAN'T SING R SONG / M.FRANTI (M.FRANTI,C.YOUNG)	◆ SPEARHEAD / (C) (T) (V) (X) CAPITOL 58629	75
76	—	—	1	IF I COULD CHANGE (FROM "I'M BOUT IT") / D.J.DARYL (MO B. DICK,O'DELL,HAPPY)	◆ MASTER P FEAT. STEADY MOBB'N, MIA X, MO B. DICK & O'DELL / (C) (D) (T) NO LIMIT 53273/PRIORITY	76
77	69	62	15	THINGS'LL NEVER CHANGE/RAPPER'S BALL / M.MOSLEY,F.OJETUNDE,ANT BANKS (E.STEVENS,M.MOSLEY,F.OJETUNDE,B.HORNSBY,A.BANKS,T.SHAW,K.HAILEY)	◆ E-40 FEATURING BO-ROCK / (C) (D) (T) (X) SICK WID' IT 42436/JIVE	19
78	91	—	2	JUST ANOTHER CASE / YOGI (J.GRAHAM,C.SANTIAGO,S.SWAN,K.SWAN,R.BAILEY,R.CLARK,K.WILLIAMS,R.WALTERS)	◆ CRU FEATURING SLICK RICK / (M) (T) (X) VIOLATOR/DEF JAM 537857*/MERCURY	78
79	79	—	2	I GAVE YOU EVERYTHING / E.O'LOUGHLIN,C.BRANCH,I.CHEVERE (D.LEWIS,N.GRAHAM,W.HECTOR)	◆ 4PM / (C) (D) (T) NEXT PLATEAU 1422	79
80	80	80	4	SPARKLE / D'ANGELO,S.STONE (A.LOCKETT,L.BLACKMON)	◆ TWICE / (C) (D) SILAS 55256/MCA	80
81	71	54	20	GET UP / C.KENT,MR.SEX (MR. CHEEKS,F.TAH)	◆ LOST BOYZ / (C) (D) (T) UNIVERSAL 56032	31
82	72	58	9	WEEKEND THANG / E.SERMON (A.HUNTER,E.SERMON)	◆ ALFONZO HUNTER / (C) (D) (M) (T) (V) (X) DEF SQUAD 58615/EMI	35
83	85	86	3	2 MUCH BOOTY (IN DA PANTS) / SOUNDMASTER T (E.TERRY)	SOUNDMASTER T / (C) (T) ID/WRAP 414/ICHIBAN	83
84	NEW ▶		1	FULTON ST. / ASE ONE (H.MARABLE,D.CLEAR,G.MARIUS,D.RIVERS,T.RILEY,A.SMITH,R.WELLS)	◆ LESCHEA / (C) (D) (T) WARNER BROS. 17572	84
85	70	70	18	THE CYPHER: PART 3 / F.CUTLASS (F.MALAVE,C.CURRY,L.WILLIAMS,M.HALL,A.HARDY,G.DUKE,B.MILLER,L.CHANCELER)	◆ FRANKIE CUTLASS FEAT. CRAIG G., ROXANNE SHANTE, BIZ MARKIE & BIG DADDY KANE / (C) (D) (T) VIOLATOR 1576/RELATIVITY	70
86	83	77	12	SAY... IF YOU FEEL ALRIGHT / J.JAM,T.LEWIS (J.HARRIS III,T.LEWIS,C.WATERS,M.WHITE,A.MCKAY,A.WILLIS)	◆ CRYSTAL WATERS / (C) (D) (T) (V) MERCURY 578943	52
87	87	87	4	I DON'T KNOW (FROM "SPRUNG") / M.STEWART,J.RHONE,O.HAYNES (R.SCRIVENS,K-BORNE,M.STEWART,H.TATE,A.TATE,J.TATE,M.RICHMOND,J.RHONE)	◆ NEXT LEVEL FEATURING K-BORNE / (C) (D) (T) PMP 64807/LOUD	87
88	81	73	15	WATCH ME DO MY THING (FROM "ALL THAT") / C.STOKES,C.CUENI (C.STOKES,C.CUENI,KEL)	◆ IMMATURE FEAT. SMOOTH AND ED FROM GOOD BURGER / (C) (D) (T) LOUD 64737	16
89	89	94	3	TIGHT TEAM / BUCKWILD (SHAMUS,FLU)	SHAMUS FEATURING FLU / (C) (T) (X) RAW TRACK 1297	89
90	73	67	8	YOU BRING THE SUNSHINE / JON-JOHN (BABYFACE,J.J.ROBINSON)	◆ GINA THOMPSON / (C) (D) (V) MERCURY 574138	53
91	86	81	15	YOU WILL RISE / SWEETBACK (A.HALE,A.LARRIEUX,S.MATTHEWMAN,P.DENMAN)	◆ SWEETBACK FEATURING AMEL LARRIEUX / (C) (D) (T) EPIC 78509	42
92	88	85	11	DO THE DAMN THING / D.HOBBS (D.HOBBS,M.ROSS,C. WONG WON)	◆ THE 2 LIVE CREW / (C) (D) (T) LIL' JOE 893	75
93	82	91	6	DON'T GO / R.WHITE (JELLIE)	◆ JELLIE / (C) (D) (T) WHEY OWWT 1105	82
94	58	69	8	BILL / J.LEWIS (J.LEWIS)	◆ PEGGY SCOTT-ADAMS / (C) (V) MISS BUTCH 2208/MARDI GRAS	50
95	NEW ▶		1	SHOOKIE SHOOKIE (GIMME SOME OF YOUR SWEET COOKIE) / N.HODGE (N.HODGE,G.ALSTON,W.COTTON,S.JOHNSON)	◆ THE GABLZ / (C) (D) WARNER BROS. 17594	95
96	94	—	2	RUNAWAY / [illegible]	◆ NUYORICAN SOUL FEATURING INDIA / [illegible]	94
97	92	84	4	W[illegible] / R.[illegible]	[illegible]	[illegible]
98	84	78	7	M[illegible] / DJ PREMIER (K.J.DAVIS,C.MARTIN)	[illegible] / (C) (T) (X) PAYDAY/LONDON 531100/ISLAND	78
99	90	97	7	MOVE IT IN MOVE IT OUT / ROCKWILDER (D.DOUGLAS,W.WALKER,J.PARKER,S.WILLIAMS,D.COUTRYER,J.NELOSN)	◆ DERELECT CAMP / (C) (D) (T) NEXT PLATEAU 1435	72
100	98	79	11	HIP-HOPERA / W.JEAN,L.HILL (R.PRICE,N.JEAN,L.HILL,S.MICHEL,I.WILLIAMS)	◆ BOUNTY KILLER FEATURING THE FUGEES / (C) (D) (T) BLUNT/VP 1464/TVT	54

Biggie tops the charts, May 1997.

◯ Records with the greatest airplay and sales gains this week. Greatest Gainer/Sales and Greatest Gainer/Airplay are awarded, respectively, for the largest sales and airplay increases among singles below the top 20. ◆ Videoclip availability. ● Recording Industry Assn. Of America (RIAA) certification for sales of 500,000 units. ▲ RIAA certification for sales of 1 million units, with additional million indicated by a numeral following the symbol. Catalog number is for cassette single. *Asterisk indicates catalog number is for cassette maxi-single; regular cassette single unavailable. (C) Cassette single availability. (D) CD single availability. (M) Cassette maxi-single availability. (T) Vinyl maxi-single availability. (V) Vinyl single availability. (X) CD maxi-single availability.

© 1997, Billboard/BPI Communications.

Chapter 5 FEUDS

AND MURDER

2PAC

It wasn't a declaration of war; it was holocaust. *"So I fucked your bitch, you fat motherfucker."* "Hit 'Em Up" is obscene and brutal—the most direct and damning diss in rap history. Listening to it is like watching Rambo murder Russians with semi-automatics, collect the corpses, and burn them in a poisonous funeral pyre.

"Hit 'Em Up" is the creed and fuel of killers. They would snuff out your life too, if you shouted "2Pac sucks." It would be like calling out fire in a crowded room. The bar brawl equivalent of just add water. 2Pac inspires the same irrational fervor given to sports, religion, and politics. Passion for his music stems from your most atavistic emotions. He turns people into cavemen, possessed by rage, jealousy, power, sadness, and lust. It is a call that cuts across all races and creeds. It slices into the primordial kill-or-be-killed savannah creases of your brain.

You can see it all in "Hit 'Em Up." This is no holds barred, and nothing is held back. No ammunition is spared for the next clash. 2Pac bragged that he had a military state of mind; the branch was marine. Fights usually start with shoves. 2Pac came out throwing haymakers. He would fight until the last breath. White flags were laughable. He is the patron saint of the temporarily insane. People loved him because he was the only person crazier than them. A 2Pac fan is the worst person to fuck with. They hold grudges for life. A minor altercation is apt to end with stab wounds and a house burned to ashes. I'd bet he was Lisa "Left Eye" Lopes' favorite rapper.

Examine the reaction on the YouTube page for the censored version of "Hit 'Em Up." A decade and half after his death, the first comment reads, "What's the fucking point in posting this track censored, just take it down . . . it's an insult to this great man." The next one reads: "Don't ever disrespect 2Pac [sic] by censoring his songs. 2Pac said 'I will start talking clean when the worlds [sic] starts getting clean.' Just cuz corrupt, fucking, pretentious government and society wants us to talk clean . . . they turn around and act like fucking dirtbags." So, yeah.

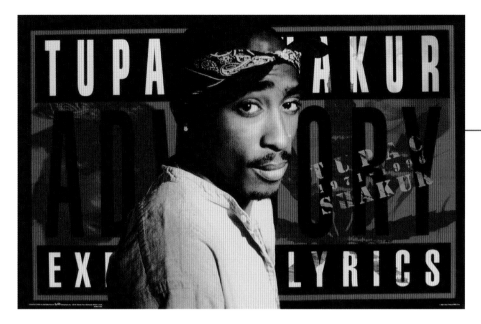

Not only was Biggie a fat motherfucker, but 2Pac fucked his bitch. This is what he told us and almost twenty years later, it doesn't matter whether it happened or not. The myth is often more resonant than the truth. It mirrors the carnal sin of Western lit's original blood vendetta. Forget that you read it in English class: the *Iliad* is just a very poetic way of telling the story of one famous guy fucking another fat famous guy's girl—plus the scorched-earth warfare that ensued.

"I wanted to get out the game . . . and [Bad Boy wanted to] dirty up my memory . . . and everything I worked for. . . . It made me wanna come back and be more relentless to destroy who used to be my comrades and homeboys . . . . These guys were my closest clique," Tupac told Sway on the KMEL *Wake Up Show* in April 1996—five months before he was shot and around the time he recorded "Hit 'Em Up."

***

Nearly two decades later, "Hit 'Em Up" has lost none of its power, even though the details are practically incidental. Do you really need a full rehash of who said what and who fucked whom? You use the song as a battery of pure malevolence; it is a heartless execution. Every generation yields its own arsenal of goons, but no one member of that arsenal has ever possessed such intelligence, humor, viciousness, and sheer rage.

Watch the video. A snarling snake-bit 2Pac leers at a sloth-like Biggie and a minstrel doppelganger of Puff. Lil' Kim is caricatured as a whore. Fires rage in front of a flame-retardant 2Pac. He tells Biggie underling Lil Cease that he'll cut him into pieces. He calls Lil' Kim ugly and snatches her impersonator's wig off. He's shirtless and doing panther leaps against a blue screen. He is athletic, virile, and vicious. With Biggie, menace lurked

> "Tupac is more relevant than ever. I think his legacy will never tarnish, his emotion is still unmatched. He brought a street and thug point of view, but his intelligence is something we never speak about enough. I think we need to make sure we express that Tupac was a very intelligent, great speaker."
> — Rick Ross, to TheBoombox.com

in his hulking frame and undertaker's eyes. His broadsides are implicit and ambiguous. But with 2Pac, there was no subterfuge. He was calling out every name. You believed that not only would he shoot you, there would be no emotional conflict in the process.

No matter how much thug passion you have sipped, you cannot dismiss Biggie's disses. "Who Shot Ya?" "Kick In The Door," and "You're Nobody (Til Somebody Kills You)" are savage, witty, and immaculately constructed. But they are mannered—polished until the fury has dulled. Biggie operates with stylistic remove; he is the meditative killer, creeping while you sleeping. With 2Pac, you didn't wake up next to a horse's head. You just didn't wake up.

Biggie is the murder mystery equivalent of *The Big Sleep*—you never know the killer. 2Pac is a propaganda film. No wonder he knocked out the Hughes Brothers and feuded with John Singleton. He was the triumph of will.

"I ain't got no motherfucking friends."

This is actually how "Hit 'Em Up" starts. No one really remembers that part because fucking your rival's woman tends to overshadow alienation as a takeaway point. But it reveals exactly how deep Tupac had descended into his rabid rabbit hole. Not only did the fearsome gang-affiliated Death Row crew surround him, but he also had his own set, The Outlawz. Yet he claims no friends, even though half of "Hit 'Em Up" consists of his "little homies" (the Outlawz) riding out on Biggie.

When 2Pac returns midway through the song, it's to dispense more artillery—the memory of Sun Tzu fresh on his mind. His tactics are straight out of *The Art of War*: "You may advance and be absolutely irresistible, if you make for the enemy's weak points." He understood that Biggie had him beat on lyrical craft, flow, and narrative ability. But no one had more style, fury, or charm. So 2Pac mocks his rival's obesity and reminds him it's "all about Versace." He dances around shirtless and shredded. 2Pac was far from the first ladies' man rapper in Italian-made threads, but he was the most iconic.

In interviews, Biggie and Puffy made sure to stress that their beef was only with Tupac and Death Row. But Pac wanted to decimate the entire East Coast—later sucking Nas and Jay-Z into the feud on "Intro/Bomb First (My Second Reply)" from his posthumous Makaveli album.

"You can't disrespect the peace treaty. That's just like when the Indians made deals with the white dudes and they would just come and rape their women and shoot 'em up and leave. Of course, the Indians aren't gonna love white people no more. They're gonna want to kick up some dust until people think about it and re-negotiate the terms of the treaty and that's where this East Coast–West Coast stuff is at right now," Tupac told Sway. "I love the East Coast, but they have to understand you just can't be saying shit about us and think we're not gonna take it personally. You just can't be calling us fakers and pretenders and non-creative and say we can't freestyle, and we just sit back and say 'nah, it's cool, 'cause we love them because they started hip-hop.'"

The end of "Hit 'Em Up" is a toxic free-for-all of fuck you's. He taunts Prodigy from Mobb Deep for suffering from sickle cell. He disses Chino XL for no clear-cut reason. He challenges anyone from New York who wants to bring it and adds, "Fuck you and your motherfucking mama." This is Sherman's march to the sea in song form. Hannibal salting the earth. Rap wars had gotten vicious, but no one had ever tried to decimate an entire region. (Tim Dog's "Fuck Compton" doesn't count.)

I'm not going to tell you that 2Pac wasn't paranoid. For all the blistering attacks and blunts, he remained self-aware amidst the chaos. In that same *Wake Up Show* interview, he described himself as "nervous . . . paranoid. I

just got out of jail. I've been shot, cheated, lied, and framed and I just don't know how to deal with so many people giving me that much affection. I never had that in my life. . . . Try to understand it and see it for what it is."

So attempt to get into the mind of 2Pac. Incubated in incarceration, born to a Black Panther strung out on crack, and shipped all over the country in a vain search for stability. By the time he was legally old enough to swill Alizé, he was the country's most controversial rapper, a movie star, and under constant scrutiny and unwanted attention from the authorities. His father figure was a criminal. He had been set up and betrayed during his sexual assault trial by people he trusted. Then he was shot during a "botched robbery" that

Tupac in the courthouse hallway after his arrest for sexual assault. He was sentenced to 1½ to 4½ years in prison. PHOTO BY KIMBERLY BUTLER / TIME LIFE PICTURES / GETTY IMAGES

seemed like an assassination attempt straight out of *Julius Caesar*. What would you think if you were in jail, rumored to have been raped, and then your former ally comes out with a song called "Who Shot Ya?," in which he sneers: "You rewind this, Bad Boy's behind this."

With his fearless reprisals, 2Pac knew that he was inviting death. Telling the world that your foe "ain't shit but a faker" is usually not a recipe for longevity. But there was no enemy too large, and that made him a martyr for anyone with battles to fight.

The beef with Biggie was the revenge of anyone who felt unfairly persecuted and betrayed. 2Pac was the surrogate for anyone who felt slept-on or snubbed. He was the wrong man to fuck with. Biggie's attacks give you the chills and make you press rewind. But 2Pac's were audible PCP. Listen to them on the right wrong day and they can give you the strength to lift a car.

2PAC'S TEN GREATEST RIVALS

1. Notorious B.I.G.

2. Dr. Dre

3. Mobb Deep

4. Jay-Z

5. C. Delores Tucker

6. Puff Daddy

7. Miscellaneous Mark-Ass Busters

8. LL Cool J

9. Nas

10. Skeezers

C. Delores Tucker at a news conference in 1996. Tucker unsuccessfully sued Tupac's estate for $10 million, citing emotional distress caused by lyrics from "How Do U Want It" (sample: "C. Delores Tucker you's a motherfucker").
PHOTO BY RON EDMONDS / ASSOCIATE PRESS

BIGGIE

Artists have a thousand ways to settle scores. Ernest Hemingway wrote an entire novel, *The Torrents of Spring*, to savage and spoof his friend and mentor Sherwood Anderson. George Lucas named a villain in *Willow* after film critic Pauline Kael. George Orwell never let the world forget that Salvador Dalí, the easy, breezy Surrealist provocateur, painter of melting clocks, icon of so-called arty dorm rooms everywhere, was a not-so-secret supporter of fascist Spanish dictator and Hitler ally Francisco Franco. But outside of a few drunken fistfights and spouse swaps, artists tend to keep their grudges confined to their professional medium. Writers get mad and write about it. Painters get mad and paint. Singers get mad and sing.

I mention these historical examples to give context to the unprecedented events between 1994 and 1997. In those years, a friendship forged between two emerging MCs with much in common, then disintegrated into contempt, paranoia, artistic fury, and, finally, fatal violence.

Claims that The Notorious B.I.G. was directly responsible for the death of Tupac or that the followers of Tupac were directly responsible for the death of Biggie are impossible to prove. A cottage industry of conspiracies and half truths has blossomed in the years since the deaths of Shakur in 1996 and Wallace in 1997. Notable journalist Chuck Philips at the *L.A. Times* sourced FBI documents in his massive 2008 investigation on Tupac's 1994 shooting in which he claimed that Shakur's beating was commissioned by an associate of Sean Combs', James Rosemond—better known as Jimmy Henchman. Those FBI documents were later discovered to be fakes, and while Philips relied largely on interviews in his piece ("An Attack on Tupac Shakur Launched a Hip-Hop War"), the damage had been done. (Philips claimed in his 2012 personal history piece for the *Village Voice Blogs* that it was an editorial choice to base the article on the specious FBI-302 forms. Furthermore, Philips says that Henchman took exception to his article and launched "a coordinated personal attack against me that dominated the

Internet for weeks . . . his lawyer badgered my bosses at the *Times* with menacing calls. He Fed-Exed lawsuits he threatened to file, but never did. . . . The *Times* caved into his bullying.")

Philips' story is certainly one of the most dramatic examples of blowback, but not the only one. The spectacle of the murders has empowered those who would make a buck off the deaths of young black men. The myths and conspiracies have also distracted from the events' reality. In consecutive years, the two dominant artists of an era were killed. They were killed because competing commercial forces in the hip-hop universe had inflamed a personal feud, and unknown conspirators in unnamed camps took action.

From their first meeting, in Maryland in 1993 at one of Biggie's performances, until Tupac's November 1994 shooting in New York City's Quad Studios, they had been friends and allies in the ways that artists who emerge alongside each other can be. Their life stories complemented each other: Shakur's itinerant, impoverished childhood and Biggie's solid, comparatively stable middle-class youth. Biggie's unquestioned experience as a crack cocaine dealer and Tupac's assumed thug life persona. The handsome orator and the obese poet.

In 1993 they created a now-legendary freestyle at the Budweiser Superfest at Madison Square Garden. With DJ Mister Cee spinning,

Big Daddy Kane invited the two young MCs on stage. Following Kane's dancer Scoob Lover's crowd-warm-up verse, Biggie blustered through a countdown of his arsenal: "Seven Mac-11's, about eight .38's / Nine 9's, Ten Mac-10's." 2Pac couldn't follow Biggie's authoritative flow and mere stage presence, but dashed off effective, and typical, lines about seeking "protection from the barrel of a Smith & Wesson."

According to Coker in *Unbelievable*, backstage at that pivotal event, Biggie introduced Tupac to producer Easy Mo Bee. Bee, who had produced songs on *Ready To Die*, would go on to produce multiple tracks on 2Pac's *Me Against The World*.

The rappers shared the stage, and they shared talent. Presumably, there was mutual respect, admiration, and willingness to help one another out.

Only a year later, the situation had changed. Tupac was in the middle of a brutal trial, accused of sexual assault and weapons possession stemming from a 1993 incident in Manhattan. On November 30, 1994, he was shot five times and robbed in the lobby of the Quad Studios building after midnight. He was rushed to Bellevue Hospital. The next day he received major surgery to repair a ruptured blood vessel in his leg. According to multiple accounts, Biggie attempted to visit Tupac during his brief convalesce and was turned away.

Stunningly, Tupac left the hospital to witness his sentencing on December 1. The court found him guilty on the charge of fondling his victim, but not on the weapon's possession charges. He would go on to serve eight months in the Clinton Correctional Facility in New York. When *Me Against The World* was released in March 1995, he was still incarcerated. Death Row Records paid for his bail in October of that year.

In September 1996, less than a year later and mere months after his double album opus *All Eyez On Me* was released to universal acclaim, Tupac would be shot to death in his car in Las Vegas after a Mike Tyson title fight.

In 1997, during a trip to Los Angeles to appear at the Soul Train Awards (where he was greeted by vehement boos), Biggie would be shot to death in his car on Wilshire Avenue.

The list of possible culprits floated in the years since the murders includes: Suge Knight, Sean Combs, The Southside Crips, The Bloods, The Black Panthers, associates of Death Row Records, associates of Bad Boy Records, rogue LAPD officers, LAPD officers secretly on the Bad Boy payroll, someone from the East Coast, someone from the West Coast. There have been admirable works that have made a genuine attempt to banish at least

some of the fog around the murders. Cathy Scott's *The Murder of Biggie Smalls*, Randall Sullivan's *LAbyrinth*, Ronin Ro's *Have Gun Will Travel*, and Coker's *Unbelievable* are four such examples and four sources I read while writing this chapter.

Articles and interviews written about each artist reveal the emotions and moods of the era. Important entries in that list include a *New York Times* magazine feature with Shakur and Suge Knight in January of 1996; Shakur's interviews with Kevin Powell in *Vibe* in 1995 and 1996; and Sia Michel's interview with Wallace, written in the weeks before his death and published in *Spin* in May 1997.

To take apart and compare The Notorious B.I.G and Tupac, you do, at some point, have to discuss their interwoven moments between 1993 and

2Pac and Biggie on the same album, a month after B.I.G.'s death.

1996. When they addressed each other in song, directly or indirectly, they each revealed key components of their style and approach.

***

It wasn't in the style of The Notorious B.I.G. to name names. A cool rhetorician, he let rephrased lines and recurrent images act out his emotions. The equally cool heft of his voice can send a chill through every threat. So, in 1995, when the B-side single to *Ready To Die*'s "Big Poppa" came out, both the content and the timing of the song shocked the hip-hop audience.

The melody behind "Who Shot Ya?" slinks with malice. A twinkling piano loop and brushed drums set the scene for threats:

Who shot ya? Separate the weak from the obsolete
Hard to creep them Brooklyn streets
It's on nigga: fuck all that bickering beef
I can hear sweat trickling down your cheek
Your heartbeat sound like Sasquatch feet
Thundering, shaking the concrete.

The lines highlight the victim. Beginning with the face, ending with the oddly empowering metaphor of the addressee's heart sounding like Bigfoot, the lines make the victim the centerpiece. Like a camera appraising a horror movie victim, the lyrics roam the body's zones. It's the equivalent of *Halloween*'s groundbreaking use of the killer's point of view. You, the listener, get to be a voyeur and yet the song addresses the *you* as the victim. The effect paralyzes.

All I Got Is Beef With Those Who Violate Me, by Margarita Srmabuyukyan and Hayk Nordanyan. Acrylic on paper, 2012. "Notorious B.I.G. is not just a rapper, he is a lifestyle, a swag, and attitude." — Srmabuyukyan. COURTESY OF THE ARTISTS

Curiously, the song-opening rhetorical question is in the past tense. The opening line seems to cast all the nervousness and sweat as a memory. Or Biggie's speaker radiates with enough confidence to frost his verse with a rhetorical coup de grace before the deed is done.

What, aside from timing, convinced Tupac that it was about him? On its face, the song is another entry in Biggie's catalog of haunting, image-driven threat songs. It supplies all of Biggie's singular gifts as an MC: images infused with implicit emotion, a cinematic movement within the verses, steely reserve, venomous wit.

"What's beef? Beef is when you need two gats to go to sleep / Beef is when your moms ain't safe up in the streets / Beef is when I see you / Guaranteed to be an ICU (I see you) " — "What's Beef?"

In a series of interviews with Kevin Powell for *Vibe* magazine, the first of which took place while Tupac was awaiting sentencing in January 1995 at Rikers Island, New York, the rapper recalled his shooting in brutal detail. Tupac said he first thought the men who robbed him were working security for Bad Boy that night. He said that after he was shot and robbed, he returned to the studio, where he'd been chilling with Biggie, Puffy, Lil' Cease, and other Bad Boy associates. He believed that the man who robbed him knew him. Chillingly, he recalled how all the men gathered in the studio—Puffy, Uptown CEO Andre Harrell, Biggie—"had jewels on." He told Powell that one of the men in the studio "had looked surprised to see me."

That sense of being under surveillance, of being the prey, ripples through "Who Shot Ya?" The preening conclusion to the song's first verse makes it explicit.

Any motherfucker whispering about mines
And I'm Crooklyn's finest
You rewind this: Bad Boy's behind this.

The Powell interview was conducted just before the release of the song but published less than two months after. If Tupac had been imagining his culprits, and it's clear he was, the song sure sounded like it provided answers. If you believe that Bad Boy was behind the shooting, the song sounds like an admission. If you don't believe it, you must at least be able to imagine how Tupac could hear "Who Shot Ya?" as a declaration of war.

The second verse is more general in its taunts and threats, even clichéd in a few moments (Swiss cheese metaphors for a gunshot victim). But there's a telling line that fits in perfectly with Tupac's memory of the night:

Recognize my face so there won't be no mistake
So you know where to tell Jake.

Tupac himself said that it was the response of the room filled with Bad Boy intimates, including Biggie, at Quad Studios that piqued his fears. The song could be heard as reifying some ironies of the night. One example: Tupac claimed in the interview with Powell that the same cop who testified against him during his rape trial was the first cop on the scene after his shooting, like the "Jake" (slang for the police).

Much has been made of Tupac's reaction to the song and his state of mind at the time. Rightly so. He was comparing himself to Van Gogh and Marvin Gaye in that first Powell interview. He was taking serious self-inventory on his friendships, his feelings about race relations, and his youthful fury ("This Thug Life stuff, it's just ignorance").

On the release of "Who Shot Ya?," I can only say that its timing— spring of 1995—was at worst poor taste. The issue was in its reception. Biggie had no reason to be party to or privy to an attack on Tupac. But listeners can understand how Tupac, whose life seemed to be fracturing from every possible angle at the start of 1995, would hear the song as announcing someone whom he thought was a comrade and friend as, in fact, a betrayer.

***

The subsequent media montage has been burned into the brains of every hip-hop follower who was alive to see and hear the footage and lyrical aftermath. There was Suge Knight's not-so-subtle on-stage taunting of Bad Boy and Puffy at the Source Awards in August; the fight between Bad Boy and Death Row camps at Jermaine Dupri's birthday party a month later;

Pac and Suge in 1996. *PHOTO BY S. GRANITZ / WIREIMAGE / GETTY IMAGES*

Tupac's release on bail in October after Suge Knight and Death Row (with the financial backing of MCA and Interscope) put up his $1.4 million bail; the infamous Lynn Hirschberg feature in the *New York Times* magazine in January 1996, in which Suge told the reporter that Faith Evans, Biggie's wife since 1994, had bought him a shirt; the interview a month later in *Vibe* where Tupac deflected Kevin Powell's question about his relationship with Evans by saying, "You know I don't kiss and tell"; the saber-rattling at the Soul Train Awards in March, when Biggie and Tupac met for the first time since Tupac's shooting and jail term.

***

Tupac would unload all that pent-up aggression in June. Earlier in this book Jeff told you about the absolute fury contained in "Hit 'Em Up." To discuss Biggie's role in it, we only need to compare techniques. Where "Who Shot Ya?" named no names and addressed no real-world issues (if you believe that Bad Boy had nothing to do with Tupac's shooting), "Hit 'Em Up" unfolded with confessional epithets and explicit threats. In a rough order: I fucked your wife; I will kill you and everyone around you (each party named); this is not a freestyle or a rap; you owe your entire style to me; you owe your success to me.

That's the difference between a menacing song that can be interpreted as specific and a song that makes its specific intentions clear. That's also the difference between the cool, occasionally opaque poetry of Biggie and the unrestrained nuclear rhetoric of 2Pac.

Biggie's response? Pure condescension. On then-Brooklyn debutant Jay-Z's "Brooklyn's Finest" later that month, Biggie dismissed the rumors of his wife's infidelity with a single line: "If Faith have twins she probably have two Pac's." Yes, Wallace and Evan's marriage was crumbling at the time—Biggie's wandering eye had wandered over to Lil' Kim and a thousand groupies—but still. His greatest rival had launched a salvo of rage, a promissory note of never-ending hate, and Biggie brushed the most emasculating taunt aside in one line of spoken iambic pentameter.

In the context of the song, Biggie's response to Tupac is just part of the backdrop, as Brooklyn's greatest rapper and his heir apparent trade jousts and tag-team boasts.

***

All Eyez On Me owned the summer of 1996. The first great hip-hop double album, it spawned hit singles and set the standard for box-checking, audience-satiating, widescreen hip-hop.

Tupac would not live to see all of its successes. At the end of a mercurial summer in which he, Suge Knight, and Death Row came to embody all

Intersection where Tupac was shot. *PHOTO BY JACK DEMPSEY / AP IMAGES*

of hip-hop's furious exigencies and many of conservative white America's deepest fears about hip-hop, Tupac was shot on September 7. He died in the hospital on September 13. He was twenty-five.

Four days later, September 17, Biggie was in a near-fatal car accident in New Jersey. He awoke in the ICU with a shattered femur and various other injuries. His obesity and generally poor health complicated his rehabilitation. In an interview with Coker, Wallace confessed to staring at the ceiling of his recovery ward, "sober" for the first time in who knows how long, and "talking to God."

In a war that neither man had planned, neither had really wanted, the two greatest artists of their generation in their chosen craft had become victims of the world. Whatever fates had gathered around Tupac Shakur and Christopher Wallace, whatever dark moods the men around them fulminated, whatever messages the media around them transmitted to a riveted public—a conclusion had seemingly been reached. One man was dead, the other barely alive.

***

But Biggie kept living. He moved from a wheelchair to a cane. According to Coker's *Unbelievable*, the thought of recording his long-awaited follow-up to *Ready To Die* provided a release from the interminable physical therapy sessions. Perhaps in the same way that jail had germinated 2Pac's best work, the reality of how close he came to paralysis and death fueled Biggie.

Out of death came art. In interviews in *The Source*, Biggie talked about his desire for audiences to recognize a transformation in his second record. The interviewer, Chairman Mao, brought up the explicit idea of death. In his response, Biggie spoke about death not as an end, but as an aftermath. Mao argued that the aftermath was the collected repercussions from Wallace's life immediately after *Ready To Die*. Biggie closed the interview by declaring his desire for some kind of decompression, a life in a place where "I can just move at my pace and not really have anybody movin' at the same pace as me. Or where I can just do what I want to do and it wouldn't seem strange to other people. I just wanna be in a calm area. I just wanna be able to relax."

An extensive discussion of *Life After Death* appears in the next chapter. It's a sprawling album, one that simultaneously seeks to crowd-please and document personal change. The final three songs—"My Downfall," "Long Kiss Goodnight," and "You're Nobody (Til Somebody Kills You)"—deal with death as an idea, as a concept, and as a personal experience.

But because we're talking about this unprecedented conflict between two artists, it's worth finishing our discussion of Biggie's role in the feud and war with Tupac by looking at how the ghost of Tupac haunts *Life After Death*.

First, Biggie learned a lesson from Tupac. He responded to possible enemies explicitly. A line on Raekwon's *Only Built 4 Cuban Linx . . .* can be construed as a threat—Raekwon closes "Ice Water" with, "To top it all off, beef with White / pullin' bleach out tryin' to throw it in my eyesight." The Black Frank White was one of Biggie's secondary nicknames. In the era of "Hit 'Em Up," a veiled, half-hearted complaint would barely register. The line's not even a proper threat. But, post-Tupac, Biggie goes violent. On *Life After Death's* "Kick In The Door," the third song on the album, he all but addresses Raekwon by name. Over the song's DJ Premier–produced creeping chimes and saxophone from Screamin' Jay Hawkins, he opens the third verse:

This goes out to those who choose to use
disrespectful views on the King of NY
Fuck that. Why try? Throw bleach in your eye
Now ya braille-n' it.

That disproportionate response, the direct threat, was new for Biggie. His convention had been either to diffuse a threat with a joke—as he did with Tupac's insinuations that he'd slept with Faith—or ignore it entirely. Now Biggie was willing to get fatal.

Far from the "quiet" he went on record as desperate for, Biggie was also willing to get loud. And Tupac had shown him how. The beginning of *Life After Death* overflows with pride and rage, which disappear

Biggie, by dreXel, aka Erica Falke. Part of a series of artists/musicians who died tragically before their time. **Mixed media on canvas, 2012.** © IAMDREXEL.COM 2012, ALL RIGHTS RESERVED. COURTESY OF THE ARTIST

for long stretches across the two albums to make room for other things—
nostalgia, lust, and instruction, among others.

At the close of the second disc, Biggie turns his vision back to death.
Biggie's conduit to the reality of death was Tupac Shakur. Biggie's car
accident had forever altered his life; his cane was a reminder of that. But
he had lived. His mother was alive and well. His two children were healthy
and flourishing. So, what about this darkness that shrouded his world? What
about this ominous sense that the violence was not finished?

On "Long Kiss Goodnight," the penultimate song on *Life After Death*,
Biggie raps across the abyss to offer one final series of taunts. He raps to,
and at, someone.

Is the figure Biggie addresses alive? Maybe. Is it Tupac? A legion of hip-
hop heads and Internet archivists think so. To me, it could be Tupac. There
are enough deliberate signifiers here to persuade us that Biggie is chasing
Tupac's ghost and going after his legacy. In classic Biggie fashion, he opens
the song with his own body, before turning to the figure's:

I make your mouthpiece obese like Della Reese
When I release, you lose teeth like Lil' Cease
Nigga please, blood flood your dungarees.

Two key biographic references are there, one obvious and one that's been
dissected in the years since. Obviously, the reference to Lil' Cease losing
teeth refers to the 1996 car accident. Lil' Cease had been driving, and though
Biggie never considered him responsible for the crash, he'd half-jokingly half-
blamed him on record more than once.

The reference to dungarees is a bit more mysterious. The deep theory is
that it refers to Tupac's longtime habit of wearing denim outfits. Any quick
perusal of Tupac photos shows him in, well, a lot of denim. The theory gains
more traction thanks to the "THUG LIFE" coveralls Tupac had and the easy,
half-true dichotomy between Biggie as the stylish, dapper don and Tupac as
the bare-bones man of the people.

Two more lines in the song supply direct shots. In fact, when Biggie raps,
"When my men bust you move with such stamina / Slug missed ya, I ain't
mad at cha," you can't help but hear him address Tupac. First, he seems to
take credit for the 1994 shooting as an orchestrator. The fictional shooting

in the song echoes the hasty shooting in 1994: in both cases shots miss their target. The double down is in the second line. "I Ain't Mad At Cha" was 2Pac's conciliatory jam to a long-lost friend on *All Eyez On Me*. If we take that as the iron-clad link between the song and Tupac—and I think we should—then all the other references in the song—the jeans, the missed shots, etc.—start popping like neon letters.

It's akin to Tupac's rhetorical strategy about Faith Evans—*it doesn't matter if it is really true; what matters is that I'm saying that it's true. If I say one absolutely true thing, all the other barbs get sharper.*

Biggie learned from Tupac that perception often matters more than reality.

Poetically, the song's final taunt returns to Tupac's first verbal salvo. Instead of replying again to Pac's boast about Evans, Biggie took the issue of sex a step further. He dredged up the most insidious Tupac rumor of all, that he had been raped repeatedly during his prison term in 1995: "Heard it through the grapevine you got fucked four times / Damn that three to nine." That Tupac's term was not "three to nine" years long matters little; the words are there to create assonance between *grapevine* and *times*. The word *grapevine* carries tremendous weight beyond pure sound.

"Long Kiss Goodnight" can also serve as Biggie's farewell to the rap game—in other lines, he talks about people who "hustle backwards" and "hugs from fake friends"—an enterprise that had filled Biggie's life with darkness, mystery, and paranoia as it had made him rich and famous.

The Notorious B.I.G. with Sean Combs, hours before Biggie's murder, 1997. *GETTY IMAGES*

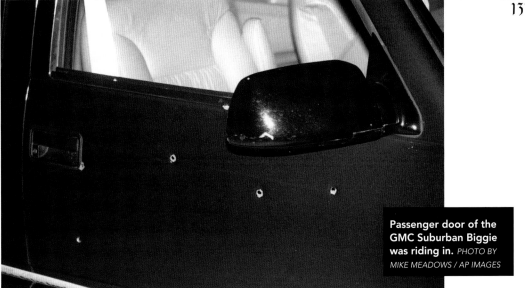

Passenger door of the GMC Suburban Biggie was riding in. *PHOTO BY MIKE MEADOWS / AP IMAGES*

The "grapevine," a symbol for gossip, chatter, and speculation, brought them both to that point. Something so simple had done in two titans of the rap game. And yet here Big was, spitting up the grapevine's spoiled fruit again, using one last piece of slander to get at his comrade-turned-friend-turned-enemy. Beef had gone eternal.

***

The Notorious B.I.G.'s immediate life after the recording of *Life After Death* hinted at the bucolic. Tupac couldn't hurt him. His health gradually returned, though he'd need the cane for the rest of his life. Suge Knight would eventually be charged with violating his parole for fighting at the MGM Grand hours before Tupac's death. Death Row had multiple federal agencies launch investigations into its finances.

In February, Biggie and Bad Boy took Los Angeles by storm. The power vacuum in the West Coast meant that Wallace and Combs and everyone affiliated with them could champagne, campaign, and shoot videos for Big's upcoming opus wherever they pleased.

Shoot videos they did. The video for the first single from the album, "Hypnotize," featured two chase scenes: one in a speedboat, the second in a BMW convertible that Puffy drove in reverse down L.A. streets as Biggie

(Above) March 18, 1997—nine days after Biggie was murdered, at the funeral procession in Clinton Hill, Brooklyn. © ANDREW LICHTENSTEIN / CORBIS; (Left) Biggie's unsolved murder, profiled eight years after the fact in *Rolling Stone*.

The clues collected by investigators assigned to B.I.G.'s murder pointed in the same direction as the word on the street did – *directly at Suge Knight.*

rapped to the camera. For its climax, Puffy and Biggie take the final verse to a player's hermitage, an underwater lounge with dancers, mermaids, and a real-life black leopard. The video was to be, and still is today, a portrayal of Biggie as half-James Bond, half-Suleiman the Magnificent: ruler of all he surveys and most wanted man in the world.

Tragically, this record of Christopher Wallace at his professional apex would be the last piece of media taken from his life.

Days later, after the Soul Train Awards on March 8 and an after party at the Petersen Automotive Museum, Biggie's entourage headed back to their hotel in two SUVs. Stuck in traffic on Wilshire Boulevard, only yards from where the party was held, Biggie's car was motionless at a red light. Another car pulled up alongside it. Someone inside that car brandished a pistol and fired shots into Biggie's SUV.

Christopher Wallace was hit seven times in his chest. He died minutes later at Cedar-Sinai.

The culprits remain free. The theories around that night remain numerous. Dogged reporters chase the truth, not to mention the facts, and may justice be on their side. But what remains unconditionally true: two surreally talented MCs took the violence of words and real-world violence and mingled the two in a way that America had simply not seen.

Slated into the more passive, responsive role, The Notorious B.I.G. dealt with the beef the only way he knew how: through feints, swerves, and verbal structures designed to delight and tease. Only when his opponent departed did he learn what his friend and rival had known, and done, the whole time. Tupac spoke directly, sang explicitly. Your words are your weapons. You must use them. Because the world has different weapons.

Notorious B.I.G., by Chris Anderson. Spray paint on vinyl. *COURTESY OF THE ARTIST*

Tupac, by Chris Anderson. Spray paint on vinyl. *COURTESY OF THE ARTIST*

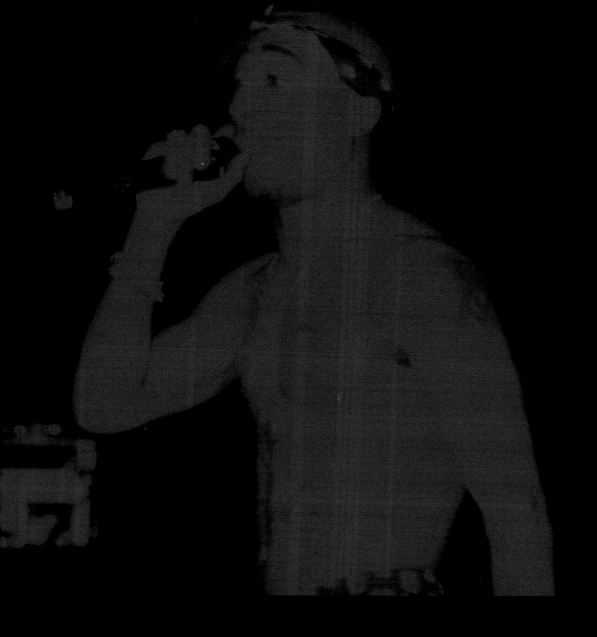

Chapter 6

DOUBLE ALBUMS
ALL EYEZ ON ME, LIFE AFTER DEATH

2PAC

All Eyez on Me opens in the ring. A stand-in for Las Vegas boxing announcer Michael Buffer booms, "Let's get ready to rumble!" It had been building to this. All Eyez On Me is about taunting fate and talking shit, taking things to their final confrontation.

The double album exists because you cannot rein in your output. If 2Pac contained Whitman-worthy multitudes, his last album encompasses the complete stress and sprawl. He is the political firebrand of *2Pacalypse Now*, the ambitious rider of *Thug Life*, the warrior-strategist of *The Don Killuminati*, the poet of teenage Baltimore chaos, the pimp of "I Get Around." The pugilist. He is whatever you see in the mirror before you stagger and brawl in the night.

The arc comes straight from Joseph Campbell. This is the ancient hero with a thousand faces: the hero as warrior, lover, emperor, and tyrant, the possessor of the "magic ring of myth." But he is not the hero as triumphant world redeemer—not enough time was left. *All Eyez on Me* was released in February 1996. His last Las Vegas night was only seven months later.

The upstate New York penitentiary was Tupac's exile, and *All Eyez on Me* was his homecoming, conceived in prison and executed at Can-Am Studios in Tarzana in the San Fernando Valley. Death Row headquarters. A bivouac in blood red. Blood carpet. Blood walls.

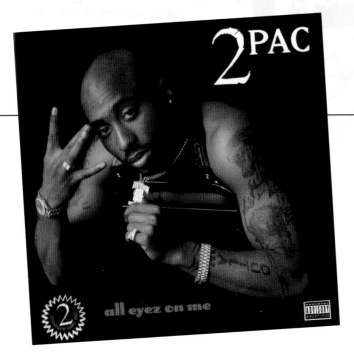

Cameras in every corner like a Panopticon. Corrupt cops from the Rampart District providing security and scare tactics. Suge Knight, the evil Goliath, smoked cigars and skulked like a reaper—feeding mice to the piranhas in his fish tank. He stood side by side with a pit bull named Damu, trained to kill on command.

This is what 2Pac entered into in October 1995, when Knight and Jimmy Iovine ponied up his $1.4 million bail. Tupac was broke and Death Row/ Interscope was his only hope for freedom while his sexual abuse conviction was being appealed. In exchange for a three-album deal, he was installed as the free agent superstar. His mother got a house. There were vacations to Vegas, Mexico, and Hawaii—cars, clothes, and an infinite galaxy of transgressions that Knight will take with him to his grave.

At its apex, Death Row was the closest that a black-owned record company came to replicating Motown. And Knight clearly modeled the structure and vertical integration on the Detroit soul legends. When Tupac signed, it seemed to be the label's coup de grace. They had Snoop Dogg, Dr. Dre, Tha Dogg Pound, Nate Dogg, and now, rap's ruling superstar. But tumult reigned beyond the public perception, even after Snoop Dogg was acquitted on murder charges in late 1995. The money situation wasn't right, and Dr. Dre was quietly forming plans for his own Aftermath label—much to Knight's fury.

For all their success, the label had really only produced two truly iconic records: Snoop Dogg's *Doggystyle* and Dre's *The Chronic*. 2Pac's emergence immediately defibrillated them from their criminal stupor.

"Before 2Pac came, everyone at Death Row only got a verse or two or one song done per day. We'd just be partying, smoking, chilling. Pac came in with a military mindset. He taught us that it wasn't a game; it was about making as much music as you can," Kurupt told me in a 2009 interview. "We got into a pattern where we'd suddenly make two or three records a day. It was so much fun and it changed our entire mindset. 2Pac lit the fire at Death Row; he made us want to win the championship and make it really happen."

The story says that Tupac went straight from landing in Burbank to the studio. Forgoing sleep or sex, the fresh-out-of-jail rapper wrote "Ambitionz Az a Ridah," one of a half dozen songs he would allegedly record that first night. The initial song cut became the first cut on the double album. It's a mission statement. He whispers ominously: "I won't deny it / I'm a straight ridah / you don't want to fuck with me / Got the police bustin' at me / but they can't do nothing to a G." His first words on the lead single, "California Love," are, "Out on bail / fresh out of jail / California dreaming."

"I went from one to fourteen songs a day, just from fucking with him," remembered the West Coast rap legend DJ Quik, who engineered *All Eyez on Me*. "I'd been doing my thing for a long time at that point and I was like, 'Who is this fire starter to get me to change the way I did my business?' He really made me figure out the best usage of my available time, and got me on a wholly new personal clock directed towards constantly making music."

2Pac's artistic legacy doesn't rely on *All Eyez on Me*, but his popular resonance does. The reason is simple: his success was built on tremendous reserves of strength, and its depths were never tested more.

California Love, **by Cheryl Rae.** *COURTESY OF THE ARTIST*

The Death Row mafia clan was the tightest familial structure Pac had ever known. Unlike most stars of his era, he had never formally come up in a group. He was a sideline player in Digital Underground and quickly cast them aside as soon as he tasted real wealth.

The Bay Area guest stars on *All Eyez on Me*—Rappin' 4-Tay, Richie Rich, E-40, C-Bo, B-Legit—were all culled from the underground hardcore. Pac draped himself in the West Coast gangsta tradition with tracks featuring Dr. Dre and the twin G-Funk sample bedrocks: George Clinton and Roger Troutman. There is no room for Humpty Hump on *All Eyez on Me*. 2Pac wasn't fucking around in Burger King bathrooms. He had moved on to German cars, private jets, and premium liquor.

The album simultaneously inverts and reaffirms the promise of the Beach Boys and the sunshine mythos. It's California love, and it's the corrosion in the hearts of men. California remains the frontier for reinvention and freedom, but there is a darker undercurrent. 2Pac unintentionally assumes the noir-light dialectic that has played out since Philip Marlowe. He is both Manson and Morrison, the killer and the shaman merged into the most charismatic gangster since Bugsy Siegel hobnobbed with studio heads and Italian countesses. To prove it, he attended the Grammys and started dating Quincy Jones' daughter (even though years earlier, he had disparaged the music legend for dating white women).

THE TEN BEST 2PAC GUEST APPEARANCES

1. SCARFACE FT. 2PAC: "SMILE" FROM *THE UNTOUCHABLE* (RAP-A-LOT, 1997)

The greatest Southern rapper meets the greatest West Coast rapper in between yellow tape and chalk outlines. The video appeared months after Pac's death and featured the crucifixion of a man who looks suspiciously like Makaveli. The "still alive" speculation increased and Scarface got his only solo gold single.

2. DIGITAL UNDERGROUND: "SAME SONG" FROM *THIS IS AN EP RELEASE* (TOMMY BOY, 1991)

2Pac's introduction to the game, complete with *Coming to America* theme, kufi, and emperor's rickshaw. Girls used to clown 2Pac, but no more. He's a star. Humpty Hump amiably mugs as the rap Groucho Marx, but 2Pac steals the cigar. Bonus points for being on the soundtrack of a John Candy vehicle (1991's *Nothing But Trouble*).

2Pac with Digital Underground, 1990. *PHOTO BY RAYMOND BOYD / MICHAEL OCHS ARCHIVES / GETTY IMAGES*

3. EDDIE F. AND THE UNTOUCHABLES FT. NOTORIOUS B.I.G., GRAND PUBA, HEAVY D, AND 2PAC: "LET'S GET IT ON" FROM *LET'S GET IT ON* (MOTOWN, 1994)

The single from a rarely remembered producer's compilation, "Let's Get It On" is a rarely remembered golden-age classic. It's also the only time that Biggie and 2Pac recorded in the same studio at the same time. Biggie buries the competition—reminiscing on his swinger days when he drove a Caddy and his "bitch sported finger waves." Grand Puba and Heavy D were also '94 all-stars, if not hall-of-famers, but Biggie only got out-rapped once in his career (See also: Method Man, "The What").

4. BONE THUGS-N-HARMONY FT. 2PAC: "THUG LUV" FROM *THE ART OF WAR* (RUTHLESS, 1997)

When I was in high school, I had a friend named Ron who drove a Honda Civic with a cassette player. There's never all that much to do during sixteen-year-old summers, so we'd drive around Westwood and bump this song at deafening volume and start fistfights—mostly with each other. He and I were a couple of assholes. I blame "Thug Luv." Between the rifles being loaded and the raps that sounded recorded by runaway convicts on PCP, we had no choice. This song could incite Mitt Romney to murder.

5. NATE DOGG FT. 2PAC: "ME & MY HOMIES (BREAKAWAY, 1998)

In an ideal world, 2Pac and Nate Dogg would still be alive and they'd spontaneously unite to make a sleazy old-man rap classic. Instead, we have the gangsta melancholia of "How Long Will They Mourn Me" and "Me & My Homies." Even now, hearing these two together creates Proustian remembrance, the madeleine replaced by malt liquor.

6. MC BREED FT. 2PAC: "GOTTA GET MINE" (WRAP, 1993)

Maybe 2Pac's best back-and-forth collaboration. It's like a bizarre-world "I Get Around," where Flint and Oakland link up to wave guns, sip 40s, and count money by poker tables and pools.

7. ABOVE THE LAW FT. 2PAC: "CALL IT WHAT U WANT" (RUTHLESS, 1992)

This single from the largely overlooked G-Funk pioneers helped introduce 2Pac to hardcore audiences. It was a stamp of credibility. Above the Law were allied with Eazy-E's Ruthless Records and helped pioneer the G-Funk swing. 2Pac sets up his shift from party rapper to gangsta icon. He'd clowned around with Digital Underground, but now that he was rolling with the Black Mafia, he'd drop you.

8. E-40 FT. 2PAC & B-LEGIT: "MILLION DOLLAR SPOT" FROM *THA HALL OF GAME* (JIVE, 1996)

Think of this as the rap equivalent of "Million Dollar Bash" from Bob Dylan and The Band's Basement Sessions.

9. SPICE 1 FT. 2PAC: "JEALOUS GOT ME STRAPPED" FROM *AMERIKKKA'S NIGHTMARE* (JIVE, 1994)

If you had this at #1, I wouldn't blame you. Bay Area G-Funk doesn't get more savage than this.

10. TOO SHORT FT. 2PAC, MC BREED, & FATHER DOM: "WE DO THIS" (JIVE, 1995)

When the first musical description that pops into your head is "funky pimp shit," you're probably on the right track.

PHOTOGRAPH BY RAYMOND BOYD / GETTY IMAGES

That was the old 2Pac. The new 2Pac frolicked with K-Ci & Jojo and porn stars Heather Hunter and Nina Hartley in the "How Do U Want It" video. The song became the second number-one single from *All Eyez on Me*. The album's other ubiquitous radio hit was "2 of Amerikaz Most Wanted," the collaborative mafia fantasy with Snoop Dogg, where the latter even invoked Siegel. If "Mo Money, Mo Problems" found Biggie stressed and neurotic over the spoils of success, 2Pac glamorized those spoils with cinematic histrionics. He relished the attention. But you already knew that from the album title.

All Eyez on Me is a fantasy, but like the most poignant fantasies, there's an undercurrent of truth. A black male born in 1991 in America has a roughly 29 percent chance of being imprisoned in his lifetime. African Americans make up 12 to 13 percent of the population, but 40 percent of the incarcerated. During long stretches of detention, the most natural tendency is to dream of the things you will do when you're free. *All Eyez On Me* is the barbaric yawp of freedom. Listen to the intro on "Heartz of Men," where he asks Suge Knight, "What did I tell you I was going to do when I got out of jail? / I was gonna' start digging into these niggas chest." Then he asks DJ Quik to pass him the binoculars.

Even at his most leather-clad and sleazy, 2Pac never forgot that he was raised to offer a voice to the voiceless. His prison time cemented his connection and street credibility. The stint was brutal and soul-crushing, but it allowed 2Pac to empathize fully in ways that had been heretofore impossible. His vision was no longer restricted to the ghettos going up in crack smoke as his images of hell. His images of being trapped were no longer figurative. Hell was here in the form of iron bars, a penitentiary jumpsuit, and sociopathic rapists. It was *Lord of the Flies* and as soon as he was out, he became a survivalist—even as his release was into the plush confines of a private jet to Cali.

You can see this applied on "Life Goes On." Where Biggie eschews the royal "we" for interior complexity, 2Pac addresses the congregation: "My niggas, we the last ones left." Even the use of *nigga* is pointed. His audience may have been heavily teenaged and white, but 2Pac targets his message for his thugs. Everyone else is incidental. He reminisces on buried homies and those sentenced to twenty-five to life, with no hope for burial. On the outro, he basically talks to his dead friend's ghosts and lets them know he'll "represent" for them. In return, he asks them to make sure that heaven is "poppin' when we get up there."

"I Ain't Mad At Cha" is equally emotional. 2Pac laments kissing his mom goodbye and "wiping the tears from her lonely eyes." He says, "I'll return but I gotta fight / the fate's arrived." Regardless of whether the narrative is fictional or not, 2Pac has earned his authority. The weight is leaden in the wounded bass of his voice. Few have ever sounded more plangent and sorrowful.

Nearly all of 2Pac's songs contain some indelibly quotable line or couplet, but it's rarely the clever turns of phrase that Biggie is remembered for. 2Pac's memorable phrasings are often rhetorical questions or off-the-cuff asides. They are murmurs of meditations that many silently consider. "Oh you a Muslim, now? No more dope games," he asks his ex-best friend gone straight. To the average listener, that means nothing. But to people in the hood, many of whom have seen friends and relatives convert in jail, the details ring true and linger long after the song ends.

For those who worship irony and abstraction, Biggie is the king. But for those who prefer the immeasurable flux of emotion, 2Pac has no peers. I once watched a room full of guys debate the greatest rapper of all time. The consensus choice was 2Pac, but no one could articulate why. They just pounded their chest with closed fists and said: he just hits you right here.

This is faith. 2Pac inspires belief in things you can only feel.

The cover of Biggie's *Life After Death* finds him in sepia tint in front of a hearse. It's a gothic depiction of death, the slow singing and flower ringing, everything but the embalming fluid. But 2Pac concludes *All Eyez On Me* with "Heaven Ain't Hard 2 Find," which presents the idea of heaven as embodied by the lust and love of a woman.

It's only on "Only God Can Judge Me" where the pair reveal how much opposites can have in common. 2Pac has fantasies of his family in a hearse. He eerily foretells his impending death: lying naked with a body full of bullet holes, unable to breathe, with something evil in his IV. Both double albums are obsessed with mortality and final judgment. Both rappers turn to God with trepidation for forgiveness of their wrongdoings. By now, both know where the bones are buried. And as the song fades out, 2Pac admits that his only fear is coming back to earth, reincarnated. But there could never be another 2Pac, although you can still see the vapors of him everywhere.

Harlem Blues, by Harold Smith. Mixed media on fiber board (oil and printed media), 2010. Collection of Mr. Louis Milano. *COURTESY OF THE ARTIST*

BIGGIE

The feature film resembles the novel. The EP provides the same taut, brief glimpse as the poetry chapbook. The contemporary cable TV season has the peaks, valleys, choral rounds, and solos of an opera.

The so-called double album stands a breed apart. It's at once a reflection of a medium's limitation (vinyl and tapes and CDs can only contain so much data) and of an artist's desire for ambition—which isn't quite the same thing as ambition itself.

The 1970s zeitgeist, the neo-natal me-me-me generation, gave the double album its formal aura. A musician wants a container for experiments in encyclopedic pop. A band wants an edifice for ambition and legitimacy. An artist can abide by the limitations of the two-sided twelve-track landscape no more.

Billboard Music Awards, 1995. Biggie won Rap Artist of the Year and Rap Single of the Year.
PHOTO BY MARK LENNIHAN / ASSOCIATED PRESS

The Notorious B.I.G. began recording his vocals for the follow-up to *Ready To Die* in the fall of 1996. His imperial performance at that year's *Source* Awards yanked the zero-sum spotlight of hip-hop power back from California to New York. The previous occupants of the spotlight's heat and light, Tupac, Suge Knight, and Death Row Records, were none too pleased. MCs like Jay-Z, Nas, and Wu-Tang Clan's Raekwon had retrieved the mafia DNA strands in *Ready To Die* and made a veritable cottage industry of Gambino shout-outs, Hackensack shoot-outs, and *Scarface* fantasies. The precocious, poetic Nas from *Illmatic* changed his entire persona for 1996's *It Was Written*, adding Escobar to his stage name and injecting a new strain of menace into his songs.

Ready To Die had gone platinum. Biggie's wife, Faith Evans, released her own debut not long after the *Source* Awards of August 1995. Junior M.A.F.I.A. was launched. If there really is a top of the hip-hop world, Biggie occupied it.

But it was the decay of his friendship with Tupac Shakur and Tupac's November 1994 shooting in New York, an attack that Pac believed Biggie help orchestrate in the midst of Shakur's sexual assault trial, that colored the next phase of his recording career. We covered some of the particulars in the last chapter—of how the rising tide of hate between Tupac and Biggie created songs, videos, and artistic legacies. But in discussing the comparative merits and modes of Biggie's *Life After Death* and Tupac's *All Eyez On Me*, biography reaches its limits pretty quickly. It's rare that two already intertwined artists attempt the same feat in the same moment, and the different ways in which Pac and Biggie went about making a double album offer much more than any conspiracy theory.

***

The pressures that come with recording the follow-up to a smash debut are enough. Biggie had recorded parts of what would become *Life After Death* in the closing months of 1995, according to a 2003 *XXL* roundtable with key players in the recording of the album like Combs, Lil' Cease, and producer Easy Mo Bee. The eighteen-month-long process would span recording studios in Trinidad, Los Angeles, and New York. It would encompass key events in Biggie's life: the immobilizing September 1996 car accident that made him dependent on a wheelchair and then cane, and, of course, Tupac's death.

The Notorious B.I.G.'s life in 1996 calcified into a claustrophobic, fatalist, black-on-black-on-black shell. The conspiracy theories around Tupac's death and the mythos surrounding the tragically young MC-actor-pop-philosopher infused the gritty commerce center of hip-hop with a note of the existential. Death was now a thing. It had taken one of the brightest stars of a generation. It supplied a new public reverence for Shakur's art, as death does for all artists taken young. But death gained a new tangibility in rap. Schoolly D, Ice-T, and Scarface rapped frequently about violence and death. But rarely, if ever, were the rappers the victims. Tupac's death turned the specter of violent death against the 1990s MC. The lyrical impetus transformed from "I will kill someone" to "Someone is trying to kill me."

***

Life After Death begins with the aftermath of Biggie's lyrical suicide at the end of *Ready To Die*'s album-closing "Suicidal Thoughts." Puffy prays over Big's presumably comatose body in the hospital, sounds of a ventilator heaving in the background. Minor-key piano notes and the sounds of rain segue into the album's first song, "Somebody's Got To Die."

The transition from intro to first proper song gives the album a central mystery. Are these a totally imagined set of lyrics, narrative, and monologues from the mind of an unconscious speaker near death? Are these songs a young man's last testaments?

Big's first words on the album—not counting the lyric echoes in the intro—detail a dream: "I'm sittin' in the crib dreaming about Learjets and coupes / the way Salt 'Shoop,' and how to sell records like Snoop." As ever, Biggie's devotion to the image is matched only by his ability to omit unnecessary or flat detail. He doesn't say he's asleep, flat in bed; he says he's sitting, not totally awake. The contents of his dream list desires: private transport, famous women, and commercial success. The specifics of these details dig deeper into Biggie's personal experience. After the dingy caravans of *Ready To Die* and his car crash, the thought of secure, professional, ultra-private transport thrills. If his old, dead rival would taunt him about sleeping with his singer wife—Tupac's "Hit 'Em Up"—then he would dream about another singer. If Death Row would outsell him, he'd hide no envy.

The narrative of the song unravels and descends from the couch. Biggie and his accomplice hunt their friend C-Rock's killer, "some kid named Jason, in a Honda station wagon." In the second verse Biggie tells us, then recreates, the events surrounding the murder. Jason, an eager albeit small-time hustler, joined C-Rock's "clique / a small crew." Jason had the crack, C-Rock the money. One night, after C-Rock went home, Jason was stuck up. Furious, Jason "figured Rock set him up, no question."

Misunderstanding anchors the song. At various moments Biggie has to pause to find his way through the narrative as they stalk Jason. Biggie's accomplice interrupts him, and Biggie has to remember where he left off. He clarifies what weapons were used and when. When they finally locate Jason in the third verse, Biggie gets "a funny feeling" as he aims his pistol at Jason's back.

He's right to be apprehensive. After he kills Jason he realizes that Jason was holding his infant daughter.

"Somebody's Got To Die" establishes the spectacle of *Life After Death*. Though *Death* moves from cinematic narratives to the freshest dramatic monologues this side of Robert Browning to two of the biggest commercial rap singles ever, the album radiates nihilism. It gives us the sound of a star collapsing into a black hole. There's light shimmering in the album's audacity, but the light travels into the dark singularity of death. A giddy tryst becomes a robbery; a refreshing visit to California fades into just another work trip; more money breeds more problems.

The album's sense of impermanence blends with encyclopedic hip-hop, R&B, and pop arrangements. Orchestrated by Puffy at the peak of his executive producing powers, the album relentlessly satiates and stimulates the listener. The sonic field of clattering snares and taut sampling from *Ready To Die* expand into new shapes. Surprisingly, Puff and Bad Boy used many of the same song producers again. Easy Mo Bee, D-Dot, and DJ Premier returned. RZA and Mobb Deep's Havoc, two new producers hired for a song each, worked with a sound and production style largely recognizable to Bad Boy and Combs. But the songs themselves touched new bases. D-Dot constructed the

bass line for "Hypnotize" from Herb Alpert's 1979 disco-jazz "Rise" before welding an interpolation of Slick Rick's classic "La Di Da Di" onto the chorus (a song that had already been sampled by the Beastie Boys and LL Cool J). The Dramatics' 1971 song "In The Rain" supplied the isolated, fizzy guitar strum for "Somebody's Got To Die."

Puffy glazed the samples into a Hollywood sheen. The scraping edges of sound that made *Ready To Die* reminiscent of the grind of a corner hustler were buffed and lacquered. The samples on *Life After Death* are as well selected as those on *Ready To Die*, but Puffy and Bad Boy's production team transformed them into silky, luxurious stuff. They pile up like so many sports cars and blunts in The Notorious B.I.G.'s newly rarified air. They touch new territories of sound too. "Goin' Back To Cali" evokes a pre-Death Row 1980s Cali bop in its vocoder; "Mo Money Mo Problems" memorably employs the disco-dance glitter and giddy horns of Diana Ross' "I'm Coming Out."

Two double albums that *Life After Death* resembles in its smorgasbord of perfected sonic products are Prince's *Sign "O" the Times* from 1987 and Donna Summer's *Bad Girls* (1979). In hindsight, both albums, like *Life After Death*, contain a decade's worth of sound—Prince's warps the possibilities of R&B and Summer's perfectly captures 1970s disco fever. Prince's genius, of course, was that he could play the roles of both Puffy and The Notorious B.I.G., arranging and writing and performing his songs all himself. The incredible tempo control in *Sign "O" the Times* resembles *Life After Death*'s; "The Ballad of Dorothy Parker" and "Starfish & Coffee" help break up the frenetic up-tempo jams on *Sign* in the same ways that "Goin' Back To Cali" and "Sky's The Limit" relieve the vice-grip fatalism of the back half of *Life After Death*.

Death also mirrors the commitment to commercial pop excellence in Summer's *Bad Girls*. "Juicy" from *Ready To Die* is a felt, personal single. "Big Poppa" (also from *Ready to Die*, and Biggie's first top-ten hit) is a sweltering, memorable after-hours jam build around a perfect Isley Brothers sample. But neither is a club hit.

By contrast, "Hypnotize" and "Mo Money Mo Problems" have ignited dance floors from the Tunnel in NYC (New York's barometer for hip-hop marketability in the '90s) to contemporary suburban sweet sixteen's. With Reagan babies of all colors and classes now entering their thirties, *Life After Death*'s two smash singles have become time-capsule classics like

Summer's "Bad Girls" and "Hot Stuff." Though darker than the beats behind Summer, the pop impulse behind Biggie's album buoys the lyrical content and mood of the songs. On the deep album cut "Niggas Bleed," throbbing beeps give the song a forward-looking electronic surface that almost masks the clomping snares that echo like boots on a hardwood floor. The clomps—even, methodical—sound like an unseen stalker walking up behind the listener. This is delightfully complex pop, where the studio choices give new meanings to the music.

The voice on the record sounds transformed as well. Wearier and heavier than in his early twenties, Biggie's voice doesn't trill the high, tense vowels it did in the early recordings. The deliberate, iambic, one-two flow from *Ready To Die* that sounded like a counterpunching middleweight jabbing each stress has morphed into a lumbering, phrase-driven tenor. Though still capable of the outrageous metric flourish (his verse on "Mo Money Mo Problems," his final verse on "I Love The Dough"), Biggie's line stays closer to natural speech patterns on the album.

The new vocal tricks that Biggie does provide illustrate his willingness to adapt to different, regional styles. Both Tupac and Biggie did a song with then red-hot, Cleveland-based Bone Thugs-n-Harmony on their respective doubles. The cyclonic, speed-rapping style, associated mostly with Midwestern acts like Twista and Bone Thugs, provides an incredible challenge. Hard to imitate without reducing lines down to piecemeal phrases with a Dr. Seuss rhyme scheme, the style requires impeccable breath control and a flexible syntax. Big had both in abundance. His effort on the disc two opener, "Notorious Thugs," captivates.

He doesn't try to match Bone Thugs' particle accelerator flow but instead sidles into a quixotic, waltz-ish meter: "We just sittin' here trying to win, tryin' not to sin / high off weed and lots of gin / so much smoke need oxygen, steadily countin' them Benjamins. / Nigga you should too, if you knew, what this game'll do to you / been in this shit since '92 / look at all the bullshit I been through / so called beef with you know who."

He modulates the stress, often emphasizing the third syllable in a chain—"too / knew / game / you / been / shit / two"—to lend the lines an integrity that the song demands.

In other guest appearances on the album, he switches his cadences to match the languid, totally phrase-driven R&B ("Fuckin' You Tonight" with R. Kelly) and to revisit gully, one-two New York City boom-bap ("Last Day" with

The Lox). He out-references the MC who would go on to become the king of references, Jay-Z, when he trots out various seafood delicacies, gambling results, and drug-czar real estate agents on "I Love The Dough." Biggie hadn't just matured as a man; his flow had grown wiser and more adept.

***

All these changes in technique and production make the desperate, existential darkness of the album as a whole far more complex. The album is drenched in materialism; any quick listen could tell you that. Biggie makes himself a don, and the attendant objects around him have been upgraded as well. The champagne on *Ready To Die*'s "Juicy" still felt like a special occasion. On *Life After Death*, Biggie does not get out of bed for less than a private jet bound for a private island.

Like every other successful double album, the two discs of *Life After Death* feel separated by mode and mood. The big, brassy singles all come from disc one. Cars are wrecked and replaced, bleach gets thrown in the eyes of non-believers, button men disappear and "come back speaking Spanish." Biggie has separated himself from the material life of the struggling young thug, but the energy remains. He sounds motivated. He raps about motivating situations and motivated people.

In disc two the tone plummets. Every single song on the disc sounds resigned. Songs whose titles or ostensible content should reflect anything

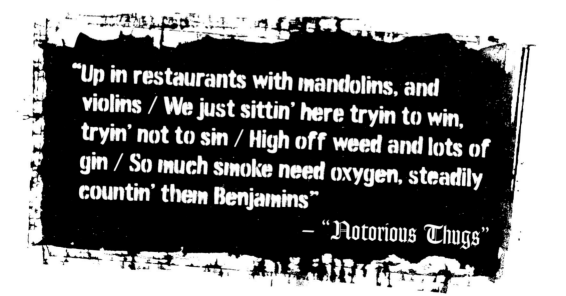

"Up in restaurants with mandolins, and violins / We just sittin' here tryin to win, tryin' not to sin / High off weed and lots of gin / So much smoke need oxygen, steadily countin' them Benjamins"

— "Notorious Thugs"

THE FIVE BEST NOTORIOUS B.I.G. FOOD LINES

The Notorious B.I.G. charted his own maturation as "getting larger in waist and taste." Here are five of his best food-related lines, from the embellishments of a working-class childhood to pop-star worthy five-star meals.

1) "JUICY": "REMEMBER WHEN I USED TO EAT SARDINES FOR DINNER."

According to interviews with his mother, Big's childhood wasn't quite this bleak. But this sensory image from *Ready To Die's* lead single—oily, brackish, cheap—lingers like tin fish.

2) "BIG POPPA": "ON THE WAY TO THE 'TELLY, GON' FILL MY BELLY: T-BONE STEAK, CHEESE EGGS AND WELCH'S GRAPE."

Every New Yorker knows that no big-city seduction is complete without drunk food.

3) "I LOVE THE DOUGH": "RIDE AND DECIDE: CRACKED CRAB OR LOBSTER? / WHO SAY MOBSTERS DON'T PROSPER?"

Ah, the choices over which the newly rich get to agonize. On this song from *Life After Death*, Biggie trades luxury lines with the debutant Jay-Z and demonstrates just what, exactly, the spoils of the game taste like.

4) "SKY'S THE LIMIT": "NIGGAZ BOUGHT ME MILKS AT LUNCH / THE MILKS WAS CHOCOLATE, THE COOKIES: BUTTER CRUNCH."

Life After Death's most introspective track gives Biggie a chance to revisit his childhood. These lines become more exact as they go—he clarifies what kinds of snacks his friends gave him. In a song, not to mention an album, fueled by the putting away of childish things, Biggie supplies a moment of tenderness.

5) "MY DOWNFALL": "EATING SHRIMP A LA CARTE WITH SOME BITCHES FROM BRUSSELS / EATIN' CLAMS AND MUSSELS."

Food that would have revolted the Biggie of "Big Poppa" now delights him. From working-class black Brooklyn to some unnamed European bistro with some presumably fetching young women to keep him company, Biggie has dined his way full circle.

but death have darkness pouring in at their seams. Puffy's leering whispers in the backing track of "Nasty Boy" would be creepy enough, but Big sounds positively clinical when rapping about sex. No more flirting at the bar and coy meet-ups at the diner. Unflinching conditionals rule this Biggie's sex drive, "Don't take 'em to the crib unless they bonin'." Words like *work* and *trauma* infect the graphic sex story.

2Pac's *All Eyez On Me* is essentially a public album. He rages against figures as specific as civil rights activist C. Delores Tucker (who was vocal in her opposition to Tupac's explicit lyrics) and as general as racist police. He turns every emotion into theater—triumphant and angelic in bloodstained white clothes as his enemies plot his end.

Life After Death looks inward. The first disc sounds more public than the second, and it is, but think about disc one's detachment in contrast to *Ready To Die*. There he just did things. He just took loot, struggled, scoped the club. On disc one of *Life After Death* he hesitates, describing actions in the general or potential ("What's Beef?," "Niggas Bleed") before acting. Violence is considered, and that's a deeply personal act. Violence is public, and in the end, impulsive, but talking about violence, planning violence, and reflecting on it requires some dialogue with the self. Biggie was always introspective, but in the first disc he begins a sustained psychological self-examination.

On disc two you hear walls closing in around Biggie. His gift as an MC is his blurring of the boundaries between external detail (which he documents compulsively) and internal state. What makes the final disc of Biggie's career so haunting is that the border between external physical details and the internal psychic state has collapsed. The opulence of his criminal wealth peaks right alongside his nihilism. Outside of Joy Division, I don't know of a more psychologically harrowing stretch of pop music.

The end of disc two echoes the last song on *Ready To Die*, "Suicidal Thoughts," but expands the bleakness into three songs: "My Downfall," "Long Kiss Goodnight," and "You're Nobody (Til Somebody Kills You)." Biggie underscores what sacrifices he's made to achieve his elevated rank in hip-hop. On "My Downfall," he raps, "We been around the world twice, all we got is mo' ice / And mo' nice. . . ." He doesn't specify what "nice" thing they've gotten. The abstraction chills: does the specificity of a thing even matter anymore?

Biggie matches his eye for detail with a frightening sense of equivocation in the next lines. He offers a cool tradeoff, "sacrifice your heart / Lexus with the automatic start." It's a chilly pitch. He doesn't say "get" or "earn" or "if" or use any kind of conditional, transactional language. Biggie makes the kind of implicit offer that happens in a dark room in a beautiful house. The kind you can't refuse.

The last song on the album, "You're Nobody (Til Somebody Kills You)," amplifies the paranoia though a final shift in point of view. While the first two verses deepen the bleak tone of *Life After Death*'s final movement ("nigga decease . . . may you rest in peace"), the third raises Biggie's voice to a higher plateau. He shifts perspective from first person to second and then to a distant third.

The third verse opens in the second person, "You can be the shit, flash the fattest five / Have the biggest dick, but when your shell get it / You ain't worth spit, just a memory." The imaginary life of a criminal becomes aphorism. The use of *you* carries the instructional thread of the album— think "Ten Crack Commandments"—to a final, existential conclusion. The implication sounds something like: you can follow my instructions; you can follow my model of craft and business. But you're dying too.

Biggie needs to show you that he's not just rapping about his death. He's rapping about death. Period.

The final shift to third person gives an even more jarring perspective. The listener becomes privy to the speech of some distant observer, someone who knew how this mafia don lived and died:

Remember he used to push the champagne Range
Silly cat, wore suede in the rain
Swear he put the G in Game. Had the Gucci frame
Before Dana Dane, thought he ran with Kane

I can't recall his name, you mean that kid
That nearly lost half his brain over two bits of cocaine?
Getting his dick sucked by crackhead Lorraine?
A fuckin' shame, dude's the lame, what's his name?
Dark-skinned Germaine, see what I mean?

It begins with synesthetic opulence, mingling the paint of a Range with the almost metallic chill of champagne. The product of one sense—the seen silky half-silver half-tan color of the car—blurs and becomes another: the tasted effervescent edge of bubbly. Wearing suede in the rain haunts—it's a surefire way to ruin a presumably gorgeous piece of clothing—but the act itself seems so casual, almost confident. This unnamed person can, and probably does, buy a lot of suede loafers and jackets. The figure then becomes a logo himself—as the speaker commemorates him, he "put the G in the game." The genius of Biggie's flow here allows us to mingle "Gucci" with the "G in the game"; they occur in the same line. But the grammar ("before") of the line pushes the luxury brand mention toward Dana Dane (a Brooklyn rapper), a move that pulls the line out of objects and towards a human history.

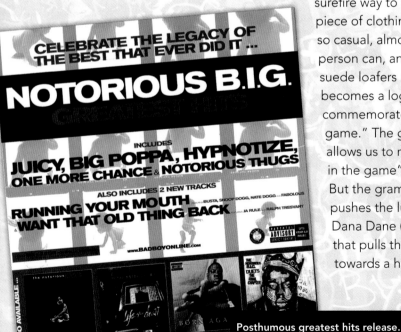
Posthumous greatest hits release.

Notice how quickly it goes from those two august hip-hop references—Dana Dane and Big Daddy Kane—to grimy, base speculation. Biggie supplies a dialogue of lapses where names, even violently famous ones, get forgotten in the rush of streets and deals. Slimy stories hang around longer than triumph. The last action we hear about is bought sex from a drug addict.

Then the subject of discussion gets a name: Germaine. The association with Jermaine Jackson gives the name a sweaty, second-banana-ish vibe. That doesn't sound like the name of a Biggie speaker. Are we really talking about someone else? Is the dead guy not a well-constructed Christopher Wallace avatar? Is this just another memory of a murder?

It's one of the most thrilling moments in hip-hop, one filled with self-knowledge and existential wit. If we imagine the speaker between the two studio albums as internally uniform, not a stand-in for Christopher Wallace but an avatar of him, the final lines of "You're Nobody (Til Somebody Kills You)" tremble. Biggie gives us a vision of a version of himself, a what-if scenario in which the MC sees more of himself in this forgotten scrub than he wanted. By talking about the guy, Biggie can reveal things about himself he's too terrified to say otherwise.

Tupac always knew that a spiritual life lay behind this material one. Biggie's music provides a record of him considering that boundary, even nearing it. But at the moment that he's closest to the other side, he, ever the businessman, the craftsman, the materialist, can only consider the physical world behind him. He imagines what the living will do without him. How he will be remembered.

Religious readings don't mesh with Biggie in the ways they do with Tupac. But finishing *Life After Death*, with its unremittingly fatal stretch of music, I'm reminded of the Book of Ecclesiastes. Like that book's speaker, Biggie sees the power of the world: material existence is fleeting and absurd, but it is all we have. The void, the afterlife, death, whatever you want to call it, is just that: a void. And no matter what you've done, or had done to you, it will not provide any answers. The void won't even talk back. So, Biggie, like the rest of us, is stuck talking to himself. His death didn't, and doesn't, resemble ours, but the conversation is just the same. *What have I left behind me? How will people speak of me? Did what I do matter?*

I'M CRAZY
Hero relives 130-ft. rescue leap

SEE STORY PAGE 4

YO, SADDAM
U.S. sends 5,000 troops to Kuwait

SEE STORY PAGE 2

DAILY ◉ NEWS

NEW YORK'S HOMETOWN NEWSPAPER

50¢

Saturday, September 14, 1996

Tupac Shakur dies of gunshot wounds

RAP REQUIEM

SEE STORIES ON PAGE 3

LAKE
D.C. pols in uproar
PAGE 2

ST. PAT'S
Stomp suspect nabbed
PAGE 3

CAVETT
Montauk house burns
PAGE 7

DAILY ◉ NEWS

NEW YORK'S HOMETOWN NEWSPAPER

50¢   http://www.mostnewyork.com   Wednesday, March 19, 1997

THE B.I.G. SLEEP

Thousands line Brooklyn streets to say goodbye to rapper Biggie Smalls

SEE STORIES ON PAGES 4 & 5

TODD MAISEL

Chapter 7

LEGACY

2PAC

"How long will they mourn me?" We all consider this question. It's at the core of human regeneration. Most of us reconcile the existential void with our offspring. They are our only hope to ensure that some off-center quirk in our DNA will thrive in our lineage. It is the motivation for elaborate crypts and sky-altering monuments. We want to be remembered and memorialized from beyond the grave so that our lives weren't squandered. That this was not all for nothing. Most secretly understand that true immortality is impossible, but it's the artist who can come closest to invincibility.

Houston Street, New York, 1998. *PHOTO BY JONATHAN ELDERFIELD / LIAISON / GETTY IMAGES*

This uncertainty claws at the core of 2Pac. "How Long Will They Mourn Me?" is what he wondered at twenty-three years old on the *Thug Life* compilation. He seemed to live his life as though decisions weren't calculated pragmatically, but were the results of a biblical need for allegory and dramatic action—the impulse to make every brush stroke so broad that all eyes would permanently fixate upon him. His goal wasn't to create his own system, but rather to create his own religion.

The murder in Las Vegas has achieved the infamy and myth of Calvary. There are dozens of unsolved questions, each with its own labyrinth of false leads long ago lost to death and other forced silences. Why had Tupac's bodyguard, Kevin Hackie, been fired and no replacement hired? Why was Orlando Anderson—the Crip beaten by Tupac and Death Row at the MGM—murdered six months later at a carwash in Compton? How was it possible that a shooting could occur on the swarming Las Vegas Strip on a fight night and only one person could identify the shooter? And why was that one witness, Yafeu Fula (Yaki Kadafi of The Outlawz), shot to death in a third-floor stairwell in New Jersey just two months later?

That doesn't even take into account the 2002 *L.A. Times* feature from investigative reporter Chuck Philips. Although a later story was discredited, the *Times* never retracted Philip's claim that Biggie promised members of the Crips $1,000,000 if they killed Tupac with his Glock. The article corroborated its theories with lyrics from Biggie's "Long Kiss Goodnight." Whether you see it as evidence of complicity or not, it's difficult to ignore the allusions to Tupac's death. There are tacit references to the dungarees that Tupac wore, the rumors of Tupac's prison rape, and his "laugh now, cry later" tattoo. Perhaps the most direct lyric singles out the murderous efficacy of "his team in the Marine Blue," the color of the Crips.

If you were to take a general survey with a single question—who killed the Notorious B.I.G.?—the most popular response would likely be that Suge Knight had him killed as retribution for Tupac's death. But if you ask who assassinated Tupac, you will only get equivocation. It was the Crips getting revenge for Orlando Anderson's beating. It was Suge Knight barbarously obviating the need to pay Tupac the money owed to him. It was two Cubans

PRESENCE IN ACADEMIA

Hip-hop's life in academia has entered
its third decade. Dr. Tricia Rose, now at
Brown, published the game-changing *Black
Noise: Rap Music and Black Culture in Contemporary America*
all the way back in 1993. In 2004, the venerable academic
press Routledge—home to canonical scholarly works in areas
like post-colonial theory and media theory—published *That's
the Joint!: The Hip-Hop Studies Reader*. Harvard houses
impressive hip-hop archives at its W. E. B Du Bois Institute.
The private McNally Smith College of Music in Minneapolis
began offering a hip-hop studies diploma program in 2009. In
2010, NYU's Steinhardt School of Culture, Education and Human
Development launched a Hip-Hop Education Center to "explore
the potential of hip-hop pedagogy." The next decade may bring
the creation of a degree-granting hip-hop studies department
at a major research university.

EVAN MCGARVEY

There is no question as to who has earned the lion's
share of scholarship and attention between Tupac and The
Notorious B.I.G.

Tupac Shakur has become an academic entity unto himself.
Sociologist, author, and Georgetown professor Michael Eric
Dyson devoted a monograph to Tupac: 2001's *Holler If You Hear
Me*. In 2003, Harvard hosted an academic symposium titled,
"All Eyez on Me: Tupac Shakur and the Search for the Modern
Folk Hero." The key word there is "folk." The most recent
scholarship has argued for Shakur's inclusion in a line of
intellectuals and social radicals who existed outside the power
structures of the academy and the government. In his analysis
of the symposium, scholar Mark Anthony Neal (Duke professor
and co-editor of the Routledge collection with Northeastern's
Murray Forman) noted that multiple speakers linked Tupac with

turn-of-the-century Italian political theorist Antonio Gramsci.
Gramsci first coined the term *subaltern* to describe poor,
rural southern Italians who were not just ignored by cultural
hegemony but totally outside it.

The Gramscian hope is for the authentic, organic intellectual
to spring from this excluded subaltern underclass. In Neal's
summary of the Harvard conference, he remarked that for many
hip-hop scholars, Tupac seems to be that hope. Neal compared
Tupac to Bob Marley. Both stood apart from the institutions of
political power and communicated with a racially, nationally,
and linguistically various audience.

So although Tupac, like Marley, blended pop appeal with
urgent social messages specifically coded for one audience
(inner-city black youth for Shakur, the subjugated Caribbean
underclass for Marley), different audiences could recode
those messages. Shakur's direct, rhetorical songs translate
from Watts, L.A. to Sarajevo. Even though Tupac's language,
references, and subject may resonate more immediately with
young black Americans, world audiences can translate the icon
of Tupac as rebel, leader, poet, and thug in perpetual self-
contradiction for their own political needs.

The Notorious B.I.G. has received no academic monographs.
No conferences at a major university. I've found no scholars
tying him to major theoretical movements. As an MC, Biggie
consistently took up the subject of labor, and he can't even
get championed by the Marxist scholars!

So whereas Tupac has become fertile ground for respected
scholars at outstanding universities, Biggie, for the time,
remains the artist's artist. Biggie waits for a brave young
scholar to reframe, contextualize, and analyze him into
academic gold. Or at least tenure.

168

firing from the adult book depository and the pirate ship at Treasure Island. The murky circumstances only contribute to the sense of infinity. After his death, Tupac has achieved eternal rumors on par with Elvis. He is this generation's cover boy for the *Weekly World News*. Tupac lives . . . and signs peace treaties with alien leaders.

Numerology theories were bruited about regarding the *7 Day Theory* and the number of days Tupac spent in the hospital. There were rumors that he was really in hiding. He was fully immersed in the lying-in-wait strategies of Niccolo Machiavelli, biding his time in Africa or South America—waiting to reconquer the game. But he never reemerged. The stories were wishful thinking. Tupac was too loud and brazen to stay quiet for very long. Despite their semi-unintentional mendacity, those stories only serve to fortify the legacy. After all, everyone loves a mystery.

In a sketch starring ?uestlove, *Chappelle's Show* satirized the still-alive speculation and the perpetual trickle of posthumous Tupac releases. ?uestlove spins a just-released 2Pac record "allegedly" written in 1994. As the track plays, 2Pac starts making references to Blackberries, Slim Shady, and the war in Afghanistan. Eventually, to ensure the cover-up remains intact, "2Pac" yells "I'm not alive!"

You can't entirely blame people for sustaining a sliver of hope. It's almost staggering how much material saw light after Tupac's cremation. He released four solo albums and the *Thug Life* compilation by the time he died at twenty-five—not to disregard his work with Digital Underground or the seven movies he'd taken time off to film. He was so prolific that he left behind enough material for six more albums (three of which were double albums). By contrast, Biggie had barely enough material for a single after-death disc.

The majority of 2Pac's posthumous material doesn't match the output during his lifetime.

(Lower left) Until the End of Time, the fourth album released after Tupac's death, was the bestselling hip-hop album of 2011.

Tupac mural outside
Cape Town, South Africa,
2002. *PHOTO BY PER-ANDERS
PETTERSSON / GETTY IMAGES*

Nevertheless, his fans were so devoted and hungry for new Makaveli that nearly all of those albums went platinum or multiplatinum. The most popular was a double-disc greatest hits anthology that will have probably sold 5 million copies by the time you read this sentence. The compilation included several previously unreleased tracks, including the Bruce Hornsby–sampling "Changes," which in 1998 became 2Pac's final top-ten *Billboard* single.

A decade and a half after his demise, it's staggering to look at Tupac's enduring fiscal impact. He's sold 75 million albums worldwide. In 2008, his estate made $15 million, and there are enough posters of him out there to earn him a spot on the Dorm Room Rushmore alongside Bob Marley, Jim Morrison, and Jimi Hendrix.

But the totality of Tupac's legacy is unquantifiable. Love or hate him, you can't deny that he's the most influential rapper of all time. On the West Coast, he was the paradigm for every single mainstream rapper of the next decade. The ossifying mimicry was only shattered when 1990s babies broke free of the gangsta rap aesthetic. After all, evolution can only occur when you break your teacher's rules.

Look at New York in the late 1990s, when Ja Rule and DMX warred for the throne of most commercially viable Big Apple rapper not named Jay-Z. From their shirtless, overly sexualized camera poses to the rollercoaster inflections in their voices, both cribbed from 2Pac. Three years prior, 2Pac had waged scorched

"This is how real it got? I just remember this feeling of gloominess." —Eminem on the day Tupac died, to MTV.com. Eminem did a 2004 version of 2Pac's song "One Day at a Time," originally released in 1996, with his and Outlawz's vocals.

earth warfare on his place of birth. Now he was as pervasive in its artistic bloodstream as rats in the subway. Jay-Z may have been dissed on "Bomb First," but on "'03 Bonnie & Clyde," he and Beyoncé pay homage (or rip off) 2Pac's "Me and My Girlfriend."

Eminem may be the only other rapper as popular and influential as 2Pac. Yet 2Pac's impact was so heavy on Slim Shady that he begged Afeni Shakur to let him produce 2004's 2Pac album *Loyal to the Game.* She assented, the record debuted at #1 on the charts, and the world learned what a 2Pac duet with Elton John would sound like (inordinately awkward).

Eminem's most successful protégé, 50 Cent, took the hero worship one step further. On his breakout single, "In Da Club," he threw down his mission statement: I want the people to love me like they love Pac. The Queens rapper perfected Tupac's blueprint for moneymaking, studying Shakur the way that MBAs study the biography of Steve Jobs. No one better sublimated Tupac's advice to Biggie about the rules of power or rapping for women. He was Pac on steroids—literally, if you believe the allegations that later dogged him. Even his bullet-riddled backstory and venomous beefs neatly paralleled Tupac's. But though his pop ear and street cred were commensurate, 50 was a pure mercenary, unable to fully articulate timeless emotions capable of spanning generations.

From big city to backwater, you can step anywhere in the modern South and still see Tupac's resonance. Atlanta's Young Jeezy applied sirloin-raw realism to briefly become the people's champ, but he lacked Tupac's finesse and charm. Baton Rouge's Lil Boosie achieved a regional appeal on par with Tupac, but never successfully translated his cult of personality west of the Mississippi. (So deep was the psychic connection that Boosie often recorded in front of a Tupac poster.) The closest analogue may have been Lil Wayne,

whose work ethic, fearlessness, and reckless dynamism made him the biggest star in rap during the closing years of the 2000s. But since his 2010 incarceration, we've watched his creativity slowly ebb. The rebel trickster was forced to assimilate and

Tupac poster in a New Orleans home, post-Katrina. *PHOTO BY RIC FRANCIS / AP IMAGES*

eventually became imprisoned by the system he was built to resist. If you doubt me, go listen to "How To Love" again.

***

Few contemporary rap stars are more polar-opposed than Lupe Fiasco and Rick Ross. The former is a slim, Islamic, Howard Zinn fanatic, raised in Chicago and prone to tangents about rap's glamorization of misogyny, violence, and drug abuse. The latter is an obese Miami yacht rapper who created a chimerical fantasy world where he played both Manolo and Scarface. One of Ross' biggest hits was 2011's "Tupac Back" in which he bombastically claims 2Pac's

"'Pac was one of the few great rappers who spoke from many different perspectives. He could create songs that the streets could relate to and also deliver your messages."
— Missy Elliot, XXL magazine, September 2011

Martyrs, by Jordan Fripp. Mixed media, 2004. The work is "an interpretation of the evolution of philosophical ideologies of these revolutionaries: Martin Luther King Jr., Malcolm X, Tupac Shakur. The colors reflect 'heat signatures' or intensity of their ideas. MLK believed the social injustices were based on money (green). Malcolm believed it was deeper than that; that power would help defeat these and that the black community needed power to succeed (yellow—envy). The final phase, which Tupac believed, was: in order to attain that which you do not have, take it by force (red). These men all died prematurely as martyrs for what they believed in."—Fripp *COURTESY OF THE ARTIST, WWW.FRIPPDESIGN.COM*

mantle. And on Fiasco's most recent album, he too declares, "Only 2Pac is topping me now."

When pressed by *Rolling Stone* to explain the bluster, Fiasco answered: "I think everyone sees Tupac as an inspiration. I didn't write ['Tupac Back']. Rick Ross and Meek Mill wrote that song. Everybody equates themselves to who they feel is the pioneer of their thing, whether it be folk singers that look back to Bob Dylan or reggae people who look back to Bob Marley. These head figures that had a social and cultural pitch to them—not saying they were saints in any way, but within their genre they did something that transcended their genre. Everybody reveres Tupac. Tupac Shakur is a great man, a great figure, a great person. He's Martin Luther King status."

The translation: Tupac is Teflon. Rappers reference him the way Republicans deify Reagan. Name-dropping Tupac is code for the streets— a way of implicitly declaring one's authenticity and realness. People tend willingly to look the other way at his sins and valorize the immutable moments of perfection. (Both are considered in the college courses that study his life and work.) His legacy lives on through the same "Live fast. Die Young. Leave Good Looking" mythos applied to all those taken too soon. We never had to watch the free fall, the embarrassing pop cameos or vain attempts to adjust to ephemeral fads. There is no footage of a chunky Tupac stumbling out of a nightclub, arm around some girl young enough to be his daughter.

East 5th, by Lisa Ciesla. Graffiti along the east side of 5th St., Austin, Texas.
COURTESY OF THE ARTIST

Mural in the Bronx, 1997. *PHOTOGRAPH BY DAVID CORIO / REDFERNS / GETTY IMAGES*

Don't kid yourself. There almost certainly would've been a decline. Even Jay-Z, the archetype for rap longevity, is a shell of his former artistic self. At best, Tupac would've had the wisdom to transfer his focus to acting, writing, and production. You could see him inching in that direction during his final days, when he swapped his Death Row chain for one bearing the logo of his fledgling production company, Euphanasia. As though to make the metaphor starker: the chain was ripped off during Pac's fateful brawl with Orlando Anderson. Had he lived, it's tempting to see him as a counterweight to Will Smith—the hood mogul keeping it 100 and donating his fortune to after-school programs and stop-the-violence missions.

All we're left with is the ideas, the images, and the music. We don't need anything more.

As I wrote this final chapter, an image popped up on my Instagram feed: it was a snapshot of an African photo collage of Tupac, uploaded to a mobile app by a musician born and raised in Beverly Hills. The worlds couldn't be further apart, but they could find common ground over the most important rapper ever to live. Tupac left behind no biological heirs, but he bequeathed a billion legitimate inspirations. It was him against the world and he won.

BIGGIE

The Notorious B.I.G.'s legacy has not cast as wide a geographic and demographic net as Tupac Shakur's. It doesn't yet have the global reach. It lacks the overt (occasionally overbearing) religious symbology, philosophic aphorisms, and, well, *drama* of Tupac's after-death reception. I've seen teenagers in Samoa with Tupac shirts bumping "I Ain't Mad At Cha" as they walked down a dirt road to the village shop. I've met plenty of people, avid pop music fans, with no interest in hip-hop or the art of rapping . . . except for an adoration of Tupac.

Whether it's because of the easy, energetic spirituality of Shakur or the impressive breadth of his output, an output with three times as many studio albums as Biggie's, Tupac has a more approachable legacy. It seems, at least for the Tupac fans I've gotten to know, that you're first drawn to one of Tupac's various professional personae—pop preacher, romantic thug, furious political-truth-teller, West Coast tribal leader, good son. Then the conflation of all those identities—the very thing that makes Shakur such a compelling artistic *figure*—deepened the affection to fandom.

For MCs, 2Pac's pure energy created a gravitational field of influence. A far better live and music video *performer* than The Notorious B.I.G., Shakur was a perfect fit for a moment in which visuals began to transmit hip-hop to a national and global audience. Tupac would literally strut and fret his hour on stage. He would pose and pray and contort his face and body. His skills as a dancer and actor aided his total *hip-hop presentation*. He kept the theatrics of his voice integral to his verses. Biggie's lines demand attention as units of word and thought; 2Pac's lines demand attention for the rises and falls in

Tupac isn't bound by geography or time—he's everywhere, always. *(Above)* Tupac Amaru, stamp from Peru, c. 1980. NEFTALI / SHUTTERSTOCK. COM; *(right)* Tupac Shakur, stamp from Turkmenistan, 2001.

his voice, for their sheer theatricality. You don't need the words from 2Pac's Death Row–era recordings to discern his emotions. You just need the violently liberated inflections in his voice to capture that moment of his artistic life.

2Pac gave millennial hip-hop its rhetorical bombast, its grandiosity, and its MCs the power to speak of themselves and their work as iconic in the religious sense. He's on every hip-hop T-shirt and he's at the top of the hip-hop nation's crush list from Queens to Kabul.

For Biggie, everything is about craft. Biggie's influence is smaller, deeper, more connected with apprenticeship and the art of words. The themes of learning and maturity stand behind so many of Biggie's most important songs. Think of the material change behind "Juicy" or the sing-song mnemonics imbedded in "Ten Crack Commandments." His narrative set pieces like "I Got A Story To Tell," which tells its story in prose conversation and supple narrative lines, contain the instructional. 2Pac had the song concepts and forms of address, but Biggie had the earthly, vocational maxims:

"Either you're slingin' crack rock or you got a wicked jump shot."

"Never get high on your own supply!"

"Miami, D.C., prefer Versace."

Biggie tells you how to do things, literal things. Manuals, warnings, field guides, maps, lessons, wills, trusts, and estates—these are the documents from which Biggie's songs are made.

"Ten Crack Commandments" is presented, literally, as a manual. It's a deftly plotted manual because the structure enacts something extra in the song. A Chuck D samples huffs "1, 2, 3, 4, 5, 6, 7, 8, 9!" before a voice, a voice that doesn't identify itself at all during the song, offers something: "I been in this game for years, made me an animal / There's rules to this shit, wrote me a manual."

"TEN CRACK COMMANDMENTS"

1. "NEVER LET NO ONE KNOW / HOW MUCH DOUGH YOU HOLD."

2. "NEVER LET 'EM KNOW YOUR NEXT MOVE."

3. "NEVER TRUST NOBODY / YOUR MOMS'LL SET THAT ASS UP, PROPERLY GASSED UP."

4. "NEVER GET HIGH ON YOUR OWN SUPPLY."

5. "NEVER SELL NO CRACK WHERE YOU REST AT."

6. "THAT GODDAMN CREDIT? DEAD IT!"

7. "KEEP YOUR FAMILY AND BUSINESS COMPLETELY SEPARATED."

8. "NEVER KEEP NO WEIGHT ON YOU."

9. "IF YOU AIN'T GETTING BAGGED, STAY THE FUCK FROM POLICE."

10. "STRONG WORD CALLED CONSIGNMENT / STRICTLY FOR LIVE MEN, NOT FOR FRESHMEN. / IF YOU AIN'T GOT THE CLIENTELE SAY 'HELL NO!'"

Filming *Notorious*, the 2009 Biggie biopic, in Brooklyn. *PHOTO BY ROGER KISBY / FILMMAGIC / GETTY IMAGES*

Putting hip-hop lyrics on the page in lines misses much of their aesthetic significance or particular effect. You lose inflection, pace, and timbre. But when it comes to song-wide patterns, it can be incredibly useful. The opening line of the song unfolds like a perfect couplet. Biggie emphasizes the same words you would if you saw them on the page: *years, animal, shit, manual.*

The parallel structure doesn't end there. The two verbs link up the craft of drugs to the craft of writing: one creates the other. Crack "made" Biggie's speaker an "animal," with all the instinct and viciousness that word denotes, but the "rules," the human system, spurred him to write it down. The two experiences are compared in two symmetrical lines.

Our ear gets trained by this opening couplet to receive the rest of the song. We're ready to entertain multiple structures at once. We've got to pay attention to the rules themselves, and the precise images and phrases designed make each commandment memorable. For instance, I've always had a particular attraction to the song's blunter rhetorical questions: "That credit? Dead it."

And we've also got to pay attention to the act of listening itself. We're trained to take the countdown as prioritized. That is, the list will escalate and the last thing we're told will be the most important. In true Biggie style, the list itself is a narrative. The first rules escalate the repercussions and pitfalls of initial success from the basic "never let no one know" (rule #1) to the extreme "never get high on your own supply!" (rule #4).

The list becomes a coming-of-age-tale that ends on a precipice. Do you move up a level, deal with a cartel and "a strong word called 'consignment'"? Do you try to build an empire while risking death if you fail?

Through its structure, "Ten Crack Commandments" enacts the evolution that Biggie's speaker has taken across the two albums. Of course, we know how Biggie answered that last question; we hear what the other side of that decision sounds like. Through the song we hear a mind in motion, going through a hundred things at once while doing something as formal as, effectively, presenting a manual.

Verbal forms thrill because they offer a challenge. What is confining or fixed can be gotten out of and the *getting out of it*, the *transformation*, is the most thrilling part. Biggie has such an influence on younger MCs because his forms were broken apart and transformed. He never let the form or the game of the song overwhelm what he had to say. The form served a purpose: it enacted different meanings of the song. It had a function: it enhanced the song, guided the song, but never determined it. When you hear turgid rap songs so peevishly dedicated to form for form's sake, that's Biggie's shadow blotting out a young MC's ambition. Lupe Fiasco's "Who Are You Now" has a clear enough subject (the aging and life of a woman) and a clear extended metaphor (what kind of clothes she wears at each age). But he decided to end every phrase with the word *clothes*: "Retro now she want the '80s clothes / No college, no scholarships so she put on some Navy clothes."

The line-ending refrain sounds cool for a hook. Terrifyingly dull for an entire song. A contemporary MC has picked up the challenge of formal structure and produced inert work by allowing a rigid form to imprison.

Or when an MC like Papoose makes a song in which each entire verse uses words that begin with a set letter, 1999's "Alphabetical Slaughter," the results are interminable: "estimating onions enlarged and economically"! Huh?

It sounds odd to attribute to Biggie the failures of minor MCs very much in his wake. But, crude or not, that is how legacies are built. There's a reason why 90 percent of modern, non-representative paintings feel tacky, cliché, and wholly derivative: because a cadre of great artists like Rothko and Motherwell and Pollock experimented with form to the point of transcendence and instantaneously inspired a legion of copycats who lacked their verve or skills.

Harold Bloom, in *The Anxiety of Influence*, argues that major writers create a legacy by acting as a burden on developing artists. This burden, this anxiety of influence, galvanizes young writers. The great ones will eventually break from their influences, and the exactness of their separation will be the key component of their own legacies. Minor writers will improve their craft over time but will never escape the shadows of their influences.

Mural in Spain. © A.J.D. FOTO LTD. / ALAMY

In the craft of being an MC—from word choice, to flow, to breath control, to range of forms, voices and figures, to the essential yet immeasurable ability to *enact drama through language alone*—The Notorious B.I.G. cast the biggest shadow, built the biggest temple, and left the deepest archives. He synthesized the now-faded skills of 1980s golden-age hip-hop and galvanized post-Reagan, post–Gulf War hip-hop. Biggie contained Slick Rick's sprawling narratives, DMC's sledgehammer articulation, Big Daddy Kane's knotty syntax, Rakim's breath control, the violence of N.W.A, and the sex of 2 Live Crew.

It still amazes that from such a taut catalog—two studio albums, one posthumous release (*Born Again*, which provides solid remixes of early Biggie singles), some apocryphal demos—a world of linguistic influence was born. Biggie used brand names as shorthand for images and moods. Biggie's Versace and Lexus were pinnacles of achievement, rewards for labor, markers of class. When hedonistic MCs like Curren$y boast about egg chairs and vintage clothes to demonstrate their discerning eyes and manicured bank accounts, they borrow directly from the Biggie playbook. When Pusha T brags about sleeping with Norwegian women, he's regurgitating Biggie's "bitches from Brussels." When Rick Ross howls about real-life underworld icons and his dubious connections to them, he's borrowing from Biggie's cinematic exploration of persona. Biggie created the reservoirs of language that nourish every contemporary American MC.

***

For a few months in 2006 I lived north of Canal Street in Manhattan. Canal stretches from the Hudson River and Holland Tunnel to the East River and Manhattan Bridge. It first served as the northern boundary of the nineteenth-century Irish slums known as The Five Points (commemorated in Scorsese's *Gangs of New York*). Then it was the Diamond District before that district moved to Midtown. Now it's a corridor of kitchen supply stores and souvenir shops. It is the center of a billion-dollar counterfeit luxury goods industry. Walk down Canal today and you'll see hawkers ushering tourists into nearly vacant walk-ups to buy knockoff Marc Jacobs bags.

Canal Street is also one of those last remaining physical arteries of the hip-hop mixtape market. Now websites can sell and send an emerging MC's dashed-off basement recording to Kyiv or East London along with some "I ♥ NY" T-shirts. But Canal Street remains. I remember spending an hour each Saturday in those months walking along Canal, stopping in the booths that carried the newest mixtapes. I bought a half dozen each week. I bought the ones that would make Lil Wayne a superstar and ones that would be the only releases from quickly forgotten MCs. Those discs—self-recorded, self-produced sort-of-albums—were made with little more than desire, hope, some tinny old Casio providing the beats, and some standard-issue Apple software used to mix and master. I would

GREGORY JAMES VAN RAALTE / SHUTTERSTOCK.COM

think about Biggie while I'd carry them back to my apartment. It was Biggie's story that lurked behind the mixtapes: the story of a schoolboy fascinated by the drug hustler so much that he decided to become one. The story of a young man gifted with a voice ripe with speech and song and an eye that absorbed every detail around him. The story of his first attempts at song catching fire and ferrying him to respected DJs, influential editors, and to an eager, opportunistic young mogul who recognized talent.

If Tupac Shakur is the hope that our politics, our identities, and our spirits can make us great, The Notorious B.I.G. is the hope that success will spring from our labor, our craft, and our wise, restless senses. Yes, it was all a dream. But the dream demands description. The words we choose make the dream our own.

Notorious, by Christopher Chouinard. Metal and acrylic paint, 2008. "The piece has dimensional wings above Biggie's head and his trademark chains as if he's looking after us, inspiring us to keep moving forward."—Chouinard COURTESY OF THE ARTIST

𝕭ibliography

Books

Ali, Karolyn and Jacob Hoye, eds. *Tupac: Resurrection 1971–1996*. New York: Atria, 2003.

Alvarez, Gabriel, Sacha Jenkins, Chairman Mao, Brent Rollins, and Elliott Wilson. *Ego Trip's Big Book of Rap Lists*. New York: St. Martin's Griffin, 1999.

Bloom, Harold. The Anxiety of Influence: A Theory of Poetry. New York: Oxford University Press, 1997.

Coleman, Brian. *Check the Technique: Liner Notes for Hip-Hop Junkies*. New York: Villard, 2007.

Dyson, Michael Eric. *Holler If You Hear Me*. New York: Basic Civitas Books, 2001.

Editors of *Vibe. Tupac Shakur: 1971–1996*. New York: Three Rivers, 1997.

Edwards, Paul. *How to Rap: The Art and Science of Hip-Hop MC*. Chicago: Chicago Review Press, 2009.

Forman, Murray and Mark Anthony Neal, eds. *That's The Joint!: A Hip-Hop Reader*. London: Routledge, 2004.

Hodari Coker, Cheo. *Unbelievable: The Life, Death, and Afterlife of The Notorious B.I.G.* New York: Three Rivers, 2003.

Iceberg Slim. *Pimp: The Story of My Life*. Los Angeles: Holloway House, 1987 (first edition, 1969).

Joseph, Jamal. *Tupac Shakur: Legacy*. New York: Atria Books, 2006.

Koolhaas, Rem. *Delirious New York: A Retroactive Manifesto for Manhattan*. New York: Monacelli Press, 1997.

Machiavelli, Niccolo, trans. Tim Parks *The Prince*. New York: Penguin Classics, 2009.

Malcolm X, with Alex Haley. *The Autobiography of Malcolm X: As Told to Alex Haley*. New York: Grove Press, 1965 (Ballantine Books Reissue, 1992).

Monjauze, Molly, ed. *Tupac Remembered: Bearing Witness to a Life and Legacy*. San Francisco: Chronicle Brooks, 2008.

Quinn, Eithne. *Nuthin' But a "G" Thang: The Culture and Commerce of Gangsta Rap*. New York: Columbia University Press, 2004.

Ro, Ronin. *Have Gun Will Travel: The Spectacular Rise and Violent Fall of Death Row Records*. New York: Doubleday, 1998.

Sabaarg, Robert. *Snow Blind: A Brief Career in the Cocaine Trade*. New York: Grove Press, 2010.

Scott, Cathy. *The Murder of Biggie Smalls*. New York: St. Martin's Press, 2000.

Sullivan, Randall. *LAbyrinyth: A Detective Investigates the Murders of Tupac Shakur and Biggie Smalls, the Implication of Death Row Records' Suge Knight and the Origins of the Los Angeles Police Scandal*. New York: Grove Press, 2003.

Films

Biggie & Tupac
Dir. Nick Broomfield, 2002

Boyz n the Hood
Dir. John Singleton, 1991

Casino
Dir. Martin Scorsese, 1995

The Godfather
Dir. Francis Ford Coppola, 1972

The Godfather Part II
Dir. Francis Ford Coppola, 1974

Goodfellas
Dir. Martin Scorsese, 1990

Let's Do It Again
Dir. Sidney Poitier, 1975

Notorious
Dir. George Tillman Jr., 2009

Scarface
Dir. Brian De Palma, 1983

Articles

Bruck, Connie, "The Takedown of Tupac," *The New Yorker*, July 7, 1997.

Chairman Mao, "The Once and Future King," *The Source*, April 1997 (accessed online).

Fisher, Ian, "On Rap Star's Final Ride, Homage Is Marred by a Scuffle," *New York Times*, March 19, 1997.

Gewertz, Ken, "Symposium Analyzes, Celebrates 'Thug': Legendary Tupac Skahur Looked at as Cultural Artifact, Force," *Harvard University Gazette*, April 24, 2003.

Gilmore, Mikal, "Puff Daddy Cometh," *Rolling Stone*, August 7, 1997.

Golub, Jan, "L.A. Confidential," *Salon.com*, September 27, 2000.

Golub, Jan, "Who Killed Biggie Smalls?," *Salon.com*, October 16, 2000.

hampton, dream, "Real Niggaz Do Die," *Village Voice*, September 24, 1996.

Hirschberg, Lynn, "Does a Sugar Bear Bite?," *New York Times*, January 14, 1996.

Jenkins, Sacha, "Holler If Ya Hear Me," *XXL*, January, 2003.

Marriott, Michael, "The Short Life of a Rap Star, Shadowed by Many Troubles," *New York Times*, March 17, 1997.

"The Making of *Life After Death*: Many Men," *XXL*, April 2003.

Matthews, Adam, "The Making of *Ready To Die*: Family Affair," *XXL*, April 2004.

Menconi, David, "Biggie Smalls' Notorious Past," *News & Observer Blogs*, January 23, 2009.

Michel, Sia, "Last Exit to Brooklyn," *Spin*, April 1997.

Mlynar, Philip, "Ten Great Neighborhood-Specific Brooklyn Rap Anthems," *Village Voice Blogs*, July 14, 2011.

Mlynar, Philip, "10 Music-Related Revelations from the FBI's File on Biggie's Murder," *Village Voice Blogs*, April 13, 2011.

Neal, Mark Anthony, "'Tupac's Book Shelf: All Eyez On Me: Tupac Shakur and the Search for a Modern Folk Hero,' W. E. B. Du Bois Institute for Afro-American Research, Harvard University, April 17, 2003," *Journal of Popular Music Studies*, Vol. 15, Issue 2, June 2003.

Parales, Jon, "Tupac Shakur, 25, Rap Performer Who Personified Violence, Dies," *New York Times*, September 14, 1996.

Philips, Chuck, "Tupac Shakur: I Am Not a Gangster," *Los Angeles Times*, October 25, 1995.

Philips, Chuck, "Tupac Shakur, the *Los Angeles Times*, and Why I'm Still Unemployed: A Personal History," *Village Voice Blogs*, May 20, 2012.

Philips, Chuck, "Alleged Ties between Rap Label, Drug Dealer Probed," *Los Angeles Times*, May 31, 1997.

Philips, Chuck, "Who Killed Tupac Shakur?," *Los Angeles Times*, September 6, 2002.

Powell, Kevin, "Live from Death Row," *Vibe*, February 1996.

Powell, Kevin, "Ready to Live," *Vibe*, April 1995.

Powell, Kevin, "This Thug's Life," *Vibe*, February 1994.

Reid, Shaheem, and Ralph Bristout, "Lil' Cease Gives Details Behind Classic *Life After Death* References," *XXLMag*.com, March 30, 2012.

Reid, Shaheem, and Jayson Rodriguez, "The Notorious B.I.G.'s Signature Accessories," VH1 Website, January 12, 2009.

Shafer, Jack, "Biggie Mistake: How Chuck Philips and the *L.A. Times* Could Have Dodged the Tupac Hoaxer," *Slate.com*, March 27, 2008.

Sullivan, Randall, "The Unsolved Mystery of The Notorious B.I.G." *Rolling Stone*, December 15, 2005.

Touré, "Biggie Smalls, Rap's Man of the Moment" *New York Times*, December 18, 1994.

Touré, "The Life of a Hunted Man," *Rolling Stone*, April 3, 2003.

Wodajo, Jeremy, "Hip-Hop Relevant in Academia," *Badger Herald*, September 19, 2009.

Websites

"Big Phat Liar," *The Smoking Gun*, March 26, 2008, www.thesmokinggun.com/documents/crime/big-phat-liar.

RIAA, for verification of gold and platinum certifications, www.riaa.com.

"Hip-Hop Education Center," NYU Steinhardt School of Culture, Education, and Human Development, http://steinhardt.nyu.edu/metrocenter/hiphopeducation/.

"*Times* Retracts Tupac Shakur Story," *Los Angeles Times*, April 7, 2008, www.latimes.com/entertainment/news/la-naw-quad17mar17,0,117654,full.story.

Acknowledgments

In lieu of a proper rickshaw parade, salutes go to my mom and dad, Stephanie, Grandma Rita, Grandpa Morrie and Grandma Sandi, Jonathan, and all my uncles, aunts, cousins, and various sinistral ancestors whom I never met.

To my friends who politely listened to me yawp: Jeff, Henry, Mikey, Crockett, Protz, Bilinsky, Boomer, Nate, Pete, Tracy, Alex, Emily, Eva, Wambach, Stol-man, Jon C., Ty, Punit, Kate, A Lee, Ms. G, Corie, Nicky, Ian, Ben G., Jamie, Ethan and Herb Gold, Orme, Barry, Tal, Taylor, Stew, Derek, Alfred, Sophia, Mike, the Gaerig posse, Nocando, Mike Eagle.

Five Lil Fame faces aimed at the entirety of The What and The Passion of the Weiss staff. Similar nods toward the sterling Stylus diaspora.

Thank you to the authors in the bibliography and to the memories of the artists themselves. They continued to stay interesting even when I thought they wouldn't.

Thank you to every editor who somehow avoided screaming at me: Ben Westhoff, Randall Roberts, Todd Burns, Rebecca Haithcoat, Jessica Suarez, Mark Richardson and Ryan Schreiber, Caryn Ganz, Lesley McKenzie, Kevin Murphy, Shirley Halperin, Andrew Barker, Jason Schaff and Ross McCammon. And of course, Grace Labatt, this book's editor, without whom I wouldn't have the opportunity to be this indulgent. No thanks to Chino XL (passing that one on for someone else).

Jeff Weiss

Jeff Weiss is the editor-in-chief of the website The Passion of the Weiss (passionweiss.com). He has written about music and culture for many publications, including *Rolling Stone*, *Esquire*, the *Los Angeles Times*, and *Spin*.

Gratitude to the editors, colleagues, and friends who have helped me turn reactions into words: Andrew Gaerig, Todd Burns, Mike Powell, Jeffrey Bloomer, Punit Mattoo, Lloyd Cargo, Kimberly Chou, Shaun Blugh, and Duncan Dwyer. Respect to the institutions that made me: *The Phillipian* for showing me it was possible; *The Michigan Daily* for giving me a home; *Stylus Magazine* for giving me a shot; *Pitchfork* for offering me a platform.

Thanks to Bryan and CrossFit Nittany for keeping me focused while writing this manuscript. Deep appreciation to all the journalists whose primary reporting and thoughtful commentary on The Notorious B.I.G. and Tupac Shakur made a book like this possible.

Love to my New York: Yorkville, Malik on 87th and 1st, the 4-5-6 train, Jackpot, the night shift at 1290 Avenue of The Americas, Rebel Rebel, Canal Street, Thursdays at Santos, Cielo, St. Mark's Bookstore, Grand Army Plaza, Bay Ridge.

Everything to my parents: founders of my record collection and readers of America.

Evan McGarvey

Evan McGarvey is a writer and teacher whose work has appeared in the *Village Voice*, *Pitchfork*, *The Michigan Quarterly Review*, and *Green Mountains Review*. He lives in Cambridge, Massachusetts.

Index